the new
HANDMADE

cassie barden

THE NEW
HANDMADE

SIMPLE SEWING FOR CONTEMPORARY STYLE

Martingale®
& COMPANY

Credits

President & CEO ✿ Tom Wierzbicki

Publisher ✿ Jane Hamada

Editorial Director ✿ Mary V. Green

Managing Editor ✿ Tina Cook

Technical Editor ✿ Laurie Baker

Copy Editor ✿ Sheila Chapman Ryan

Design Director ✿ Stan Green

Production Manager ✿ Regina Girard

Illustrator ✿ Laurel Strand

Cover & Text Designer ✿ Shelly Garrison

Photographer ✿ Brent Kane

Mission Statement

Dedicated to providing quality products and
service to inspire creativity.

The New Handmade: Simple Sewing for Contemporary Style
© 2008 by Cassie Barden

Martingale® & COMPANY ▪ That Patchwork Place®

That Patchwork Place® is an imprint of Martingale &
Company®.

Martingale & Company
20205 144th Ave. NE
Woodinville, WA 98072-8478 USA
www.martingale-pub.com

Printed in China
13 12 11 10 09   876543

Library of Congress Cataloging-in-Publication Data
Library of Congress Control Number: 2008031697

ISBN: 978-1-56477-877-2

Dedication

To my parents, who have wholeheartedly encouraged me in every venture no matter how many times I changed my mind. And especially to my mom, who not only taught me to sew and quilt, but has also supported this process at each step as my pattern tester, cheerleader, business advisor, and fabric-stash venture capitalist. I couldn't have done this without you.

Acknowledgments

Thank you to the passionate, dedicated, and talented folks at Martingale & Company for making this book possible.

And were it not for the creativity and DIY spirit of the new craft community, this book wouldn't have a home. To everyone out there making things by hand, you inspire me daily and I hope I can give a bit of that back.

contents

WHAT IS THE
"NEW HANDMADE"? ✿ 9

INSPIRATION ✿ 10

MISTAKES AND MODIFICATIONS ✿ 10

CHOOSING FABRIC ✿ 11

BAGS, TOTES, AND PURSES

Reading List Tote ✿ 17

Victorian Cameo Bag ✿ 21

Vintage is the New Modern
Patchwork Bag ✿ 25

Flea Market Purse ✿ 27

Tropical Vintage Patchwork Bag ✿ 33

Dinner Party Grocery Bag ✿ 37

Bird-Watcher Messenger Bag ✿ 41

CASES, COVERS, AND ZIPPERED BAGS

Zippered Kit Bag ✿ 49

Evening Essentials Wristlet ✿ 51

Cell Phone Case ✿ 55

Portable Media Player Case ✿ 59

Plein Air Sketchbook Cover ✿ 61

Novella Composition-Book Cover ✿ 63

Picasso Pencil Case ✿ 67

All Business Laptop Sleeve ✿ 71

HOME AND ABROAD

Pot Holder ✿ 79

Oven Mitt ✿ 83

I ❤ Coffee French-Press Cozy ✿ 87

Pocket Place Mats ✿ 90

Pretty Crafty Apron ✿ 92

Cotton Cuff ✿ 94

Headband ✿ 96

Knit-Not Scarf ✿ 99

GENERAL INSTRUCTIONS ✿ 100

MEET THE AUTHOR ✿ 112

what is the "new handmade"?

People have been making things by hand since the first Homo sapiens tied on an antelope-skin loincloth. In the past few decades fewer and fewer people are discovering the joys of creating things from scratch. From take-out dinners to multistory clothing stores, everything is so easily available that skills like sewing have, for many, fallen by the wayside. Few schools offer home economics classes anymore, and few people learn to make things by hand from their parents or grandparents.

But we're experiencing a resurgence of all things handmade. You see it in food, in art, and especially in crafts like sewing, knitting, quilting, and embroidery. As the world gets larger and more complex, more plugged in and surrounded by automation and technology and gadgets, as we become more separated from the processes that create our food, our clothing, and our homes, we're starting to miss the connection to the things around us. We want to feel like we took part in the process, whether it's making a meal from scratch or wearing a piece of clothing we constructed ourselves.

The New Handmade is an appreciation for the unique object, for every individual's creativity, and for the process of creating. When we were kids we reveled in arts and crafts. Why can't we still? We weren't told that only the most talented could create art, or that it was easier to buy a mug at the store than to make one for Dad with our own hands.

In the past, people made things by hand because they had to. It was more economical, or what you needed was simply unavailable for purchase—you couldn't just go to the nearby megamart and buy a skirt off the rack. When you hand make something today, however, you recognize the value of the process, of your unique vision, of your creativity. You imbue the handmade with a bit of yourself; a gift for someone that you've made by hand is a very special thing.

Today we make things to take part in the world of objects that surround us. We get to use the creativity that we all possess, but that the increasingly automated world doesn't require us to use. We make each choice along the way, from choosing fabric to selecting the color of the thread.

And most importantly, there's something soothing, involving, and immensely satisfying about making something by hand.

inspiration

It's been said many times before but bears repeating: inspiration is everywhere. Some people enjoy classical art, or take inspiration from music, mid-century design, graphic novels, or the art and decoration of other cultures. If you have trouble finding inspiration, be it fabric styles or color choices or what kind of handles to use on your next bag, take a look at your favorite artistic medium. You may get an idea for a novel color combination at a new art exhibit, or see a period film that inspires your next handmade accessory. Just walking around your town or city can bring inspiration, too. I'm constantly inspired by the creative, unique, and fashionable style of the people in my Seattle neighborhood. Looking through your favorite catalogs is another great place to get ideas.

mistakes and modifications

I learned sewing basics from my mom when I was a kid, though I didn't stick to it. I started sewing again in my early 20s with a friend who went on to become a fashion designer, and a few years later I learned how to quilt. But even with a bit of a sewing background, much of what I've learned in the past few years has been by trial and error. Learning in this way has taught me the virtue of the so-called mistake. In quilting there's an old practice of incorporating a "humility block" into a quilt. This was a block that was intentionally pieced wrong, or placed upside down. These quilters knew that humans aren't perfect, and that imperfections are what make the things around us unique and beautiful. Many times the most interesting and special project is the one with a few quirks. So as you work on these projects, I don't want you to worry about mistakes. Some mistakes will require a seam ripper (every sewer's best friend) but some mistakes can be left as they are—oftentimes what we perceive as a "mistake" is just a tiny variation from the pattern that no one will ever notice. And remember, this is about the joy of making things by hand. We all have enough expectations and requirements in our lives without bringing more into our sewing, so let go and have fun.

One of the great things about the New Handmade is that people are feeling empowered to experiment with their own ideas. As you make projects from this book, I encourage you to personalize and adapt wherever you want. Turn one of your own drawings into an appliqué. Or, instead of using quilting cottons, use a piece of antique velvet for a tote bag. Combine elements of different projects together, like using the handle design from one project on another. Mix and match techniques as well: use the quilting techniques from the Vintage is the New Modern Patchwork Bag (page 25) to make a set of quilted Zippered Kit Bags (page 49).

I hope the projects in this book inspire you, whether you make them exactly how I have or adapt them in some way. When you make something, I'd love to see it! Post your show and tell at www.thenewhandmade.com.

choosing fabric

Just about the time I learned how to quilt, irresistible contemporary quilting cottons began hitting fabric stores. It was wonderful to have such modern patterns and colors available. Each season there are more and more fantastic collections to choose from, influenced by current trends, color schemes, and motifs. Several designers are now offering their lines in home-decor weights or vinyl-coated cottons, and charming and unique fabrics from Japan are becoming more available every day.

I highly recommend you check out the new styles and colors that are available at your local quilting or fabric store, but in the end it's all about personal taste. What's popular at the moment doesn't make a difference if you're holding a bolt in your hands that you really love. And if you like it, use it. I definitely have

my fabric tastes, and you'll get to know them as you read this book, but you don't have to use the kinds of fabrics I use. Make everything out of romantic florals, or nineteenth-century reproductions, or flying-pig prints if that's what you prefer. Fabric trends come and go, but a handmade bag will be with you much longer and you've got to love it.

No matter your favorite styles, sometimes choosing complementary fabrics for a project can be difficult. I've spent many afternoons in the quilt shop, surrounded by gorgeous fabric, unable to put two bolts together to save my life. This is when some basic design concepts and color theory come in handy. So on the next two pages is some helpful information if you need a little mental nudge when picking out fabric.

Color. Choosing colors without any reference can be difficult, so consider the surroundings in which the project might end up. Sometimes you're making a project to match an existing color scheme, like with home-decor items. Maybe you're making the Pot Holder (page 79) and Oven Mitt (page 83) for a retro kitchen with a lot of red. More red is an obvious choice, but primary yellow or chambray blue are also good companions for red. Or if you're making a wristlet to match an emerald cocktail dress, magenta would be a striking complement. If you're making a tote bag as a gift, think of the person's favorite color, or what color clothing they wear often.

If you need ideas for putting colors together, a very easy and effective way is to just look around. Use the colors from a book cover that catches your eye, or a photograph you really love, or a favorite painting. In the same way, you can pull colors from a main or "focus" fabric to use for accent colors. If you're still at a loss, search "color wheel" or "color theory" on the Web and you'll find a gazillion sites that will explain the basics and give you more ideas for color schemes than you could ever use.

Contrast. Contrast dictates how fabrics appear to blend together or stand out from one another. Whether you want a high-impact look or a more subtle, blended look, contrast is how to achieve it. A large difference in color can create more contrast (like bright red against bright green), whereas a small difference can create a low-contrast look, like green next to blue. The intensity of colors comes into play as well. That same red and green will have less contrast if they are pale pastels. If you're having trouble gauging contrast, put your fabrics next to each other, step back, and squint. As the details blur you'll have a better idea if the fabric stands out to the degree you want.

Scale. A tiny print on a large project might look muddy from a few feet away. Similarly, a large print on a small accessory might be lost. However, sometimes a large print cut into small pieces can have a great effect! Similarly, sometimes many small prints next to each other can be exactly the look you want, just as two very large prints next to each other can be unexpected and exciting. Experiment and play with scale, contrast, and color until you have a combination of fabrics that appeals to you.

Purpose. With bags, accessories, and home-decor projects, practicality can come into play. For example, if you're making the I ❤ Coffee French-Press Cozy (page 87), which is bound to get a little coffee on it, don't pick sparkling white fabric unless you're good friends with bleach.

Theme. Like the coffee-themed fabric I used on the French-press cozy, sometimes the project picks its own fabric. The Flea Market Purse (page 27) came about after I found this adorable Japanese country fabric and was inspired by the handbags I'd seen in Japanese sewing books. I made another Bird-Watcher Messenger Bag (page 41) with a Japanese print of a wolf chasing little lambs. It was cartoony and woodsy already, so I combined it with a woodgrain fabric and a red-and-white polka-dotted print. My friend calls it the Little Red Riding Hood bag.

A WORD ABOUT FABRIC

There's a huge range of fabric out there in a huge range of prices. I highly recommend purchasing the nicest cottons you can afford. Quilt shops carry a wonderful selection of high-quality cotton fabric from name-brand companies, and while it might seem a bit more expensive, you do get what you pay for. The fabric at quilt shops has a higher thread count, which is why it feels so much softer than something much less expensive. Designs print better and show more detail on fabrics with higher thread counts. Practically, these fabrics tend to hold up better, especially important with something that will see heavy use like a tote bag. The exciting contemporary fabric collections are often exclusive to quilt shops and small independent fabric stores. Finally, bringing your business to those local independent shops is a great way to contribute and be involved in the craft community that you're a part of, as well as your community as a whole.

If you don't have quilt or fabric stores in your area, try looking online. There are many wonderful online fabric retailers who carry the same high-quality fabrics as quilt shops, and online is often the only place to get hard-to-find fabrics like those imported from Japan.

bags, totes,

and purses

reading list tote

1 Inspired by old library book bags, this is the bag I imagine my older sister carrying around as a little girl in 1970's upstate New York. This is a great first project because it uses several construction techniques you'll find in other projects in the book, and it's very easy. Once you learn how to make it, you can make it in any size, dimension, or fabric combination you please. Keep it simple with gorgeous quilting cottons or experiment with other fabrics. Cotton canvas is a great option since it makes for a sturdy bag, and I'm constantly finding unique imported canvas from Japan. This tote bag is also a great place to experiment with appliqué (see the Victorian Cameo Bag on page 21).

Because of the way these straps are constructed, you can cut two pieces *each* from two fabrics and make straps that are different on either side.

MATERIALS

Yardage is based on 42"-wide fabric.

½ yard of light blue print canvas for outer-bag main piece and straps

½ yard of solid rust fabric for lining

¼ yard of olive green print for outer-bag coordinating strip

⅜ yard of lightweight fusible interfacing

CUTTING

From the light blue print canvas, cut:
2 squares, 12" x 12"
4 strips, 1¼" x 20"

From the olive green print, cut:
2 rectangles, 5" x 12"

From the solid rust fabric, cut:
2 rectangles, 12" x 16"

From the interfacing, cut:
2 rectangles, 10¾" x 15½"

MAKING THE BAG

Use ½"-wide seam allowances throughout, unless otherwise indicated.

1. The contrasting panel can be at the bottom of the bag or the top, depending on your fabric choices and preference. Pin and sew the 12" edges of an olive green rectangle and a light blue square, right sides together. Repeat with the remaining olive green rectangle and light blue square. Press the seam allowances open.

2. Place the front and back panels from step 1 right sides together. Sew around the side and bottom edges, leaving the top edge open. Clip the bottom corners at an angle, and then turn the piece right side out. This is the outer bag.

3. For the lining, place the rust rectangles right sides together and sew around the side and bottom edges like you did for the outer bag. Leave a 3" gap about 2" from the bottom on one side seam. You will eventually be pulling the entire bag through this hole, so make sure to backstitch before and after the gap for extra strength. Clip the bottom corners as in step 2 but do not turn the piece.

4. On the wrong sides of the lining piece, position the interfacing rectangles so they match at the top, raw edge of the lining and are just within the stitching line along the sides. Follow the manufacturer's instructions to fuse the interfacing in place.

5. To make the straps, press under ¼" along each long edge of all four light blue strips. Pin two strips wrong sides together and topstitch ⅛" from both long edges. Repeat for the remaining two strips.

6. Mark 2" in from each side seam along the top edge of the outer bag. With the raw edges matching, pin the ends of each strap to the bag, aligning the outer edges of the strap with your 2" mark. It's easy for the straps to get pushed at an angle as you sew the next seam, so pin the strap to the outer bag a couple inches down from the top to keep it perpendicular. Repeat with the remaining strap on the other side of the bag.

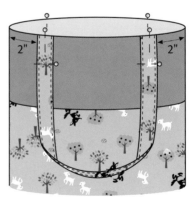

7. With right sides together, place the outer bag and straps inside the lining bag, sandwiching the straps between the layers. Align and pin the raw edges together.

8. Sew all the way around the top of the bag, back-stitching over the two side seams and over each strap.

9. Pull the bag through the gap you left in the lining seam. While the lining is "out" of the outer bag, whipstitch the gap closed.

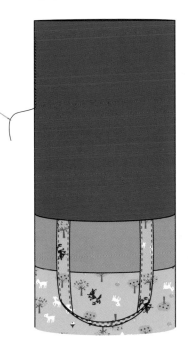

10. Push the lining into the outer bag, roll the top seam (page 106), and press the bag.

victorian cameo bag

When damask, silhouettes, ruffles, and pearls all suddenly came back into fashion in the past couple of years, I admit to being rather giddy about it. There's something about prim but playful Victorian styles that I really love. This bag is inspired by those fashions, but is firmly planted in this century by the graphic drama of the black on cream. The next time you're invited to high tea, you'll have the perfect bag for the occasion.

A variation of the Reading List Tote (page 17), this bag is padded and introduces two new techniques. One is an alternative way to sew straps using only one piece of fabric instead of two. You'll also be doing a little bit of appliqué.

MATERIALS

Yardage is based on 42"-wide fabric unless indicated otherwise.

⅔ yard of black-and-cream damask for outer bag and straps

½ yard of purple print for lining

⅜ yard of solid black fabric for appliqué and outer-bag contrasting strips

Scrap of cream fabric for appliqué

½ yard of 17"-wide paper-backed fusible web

⅜ yard of batting

CUTTING

Refer to "Machine Appliqué" (page 107) to prepare the appliqués.

From the black-and-cream damask, cut:
2 rectangles, 12" x 14"
2 strips, 4" x 20"

From the solid black fabric, cut:
4 strips, 2" x 12"
1 large oval appliqué (page 23)
1 horse head appliqué (page 23)

From the purple print, cut:
2 rectangles, 12" x 16"

From the cream fabric scrap, cut:
1 small oval appliqué (page 23)

From the batting, cut:
2 rectangles, 12" x 16"

MAKING THE BAG

Use ½"-wide seam allowances throughout, unless otherwise indicated.

1. Pin and sew the 12" edge of each black strip to the short edges of each damask rectangle. Press the seam allowances open.

2. Referring to "Machine Appliqué" (page 107), center and appliqué the cream oval to the black oval. Center and appliqué the

21

horse head to the cream oval. Center and appliqué the unit to one of the damask pieces.

3. Place the appliquéd panel and the remaining panel from step 1 right sides together. Sew around the side and bottom edges. Clip the bottom corners at an angle, and then turn the piece right side out. This is the outer bag.

4. Layer a batting rectangle on the wrong side of each purple rectangle. With the lining pieces right sides together and using a walking foot, sew around the side and bottom edges like you did for the outer bag. Leave a 3" gap about 2" from the bottom on one side seam. You will eventually pull the entire bag through this hole, so make sure to backstitch before and after the gap for extra strength. Trim away the batting in the seam allowances. Clip the bottom corners as in step 3, but do not turn the piece.

5. To make the straps, fold a damask print strip in half lengthwise, wrong sides together, and press the fold. Unfold, turn the raw edges of the strip in to the center crease, refold on the center crease, and then press the strip. Topstitch along each long side of the strap a scant ⅛" from the edge. Repeat with the remaining damask strip.

6. Mark 2" in from each side seam along the top edge of the outer bag. With the raw edges matching, pin the ends of each strap to the bag, aligning the outer edges of the strap with your 2" mark. It's easy for the straps to get pushed at an angle as you sew the next seam, so pin the strap to the outer bag a couple inches down to keep it perpendicular. Repeat with the remaining strap on the other side of the bag.

7. With right sides together, place the outer bag and straps inside the lining bag, sandwiching the straps between the layers. Align and pin the raw edges together.

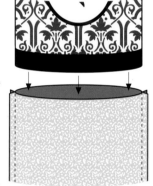

8. Sew all the way around the top of the bag, back-stitching over the two side seams, as well as over each strap.

9. Pull the bag through the gap you left in the lining seam. While the lining is "out" of the outer bag, whipstitch the gap closed.

10. Push the lining into the outer bag, roll the top seam (page 106), and press the bag.

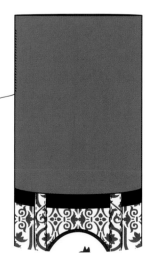

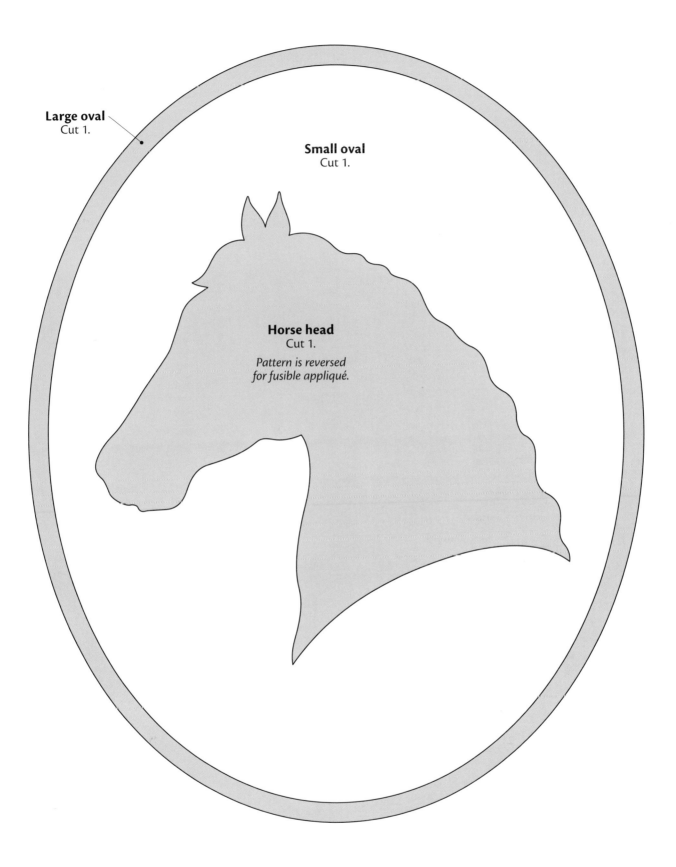

Large oval
Cut 1.

Small oval
Cut 1.

Horse head
Cut 1.

*Pattern is reversed
for fusible appliqué.*

vintage is the new modern patchwork bag

This bag began as another version of the Reading List Tote, but the patchwork and batting create something entirely different. I love the simplicity of square patchwork, and as a quilter as well as a sewer, I could hardly let this book go by without introducing the basics of quiltmaking.

When choosing fabrics, you can emphasize the geometry of the patchwork with high-contrast fabrics, or go for a scrappier, low-contrast look. For the pastel bag, I used fabrics from Heather Bailey's Freshcut collection by Free Spirit, which makes for a soft, romantic bag. The blue-and-white tote has an entirely different look. Inspired by the clean, bright designs common in Japanese quiltmaking, this bag uses white fabric for the background and a variety of blue squares, with some red thrown in for interest, for the alternating squares. I sewed decorative buttons to the base of the straps on both bags. You also have the option of tying the layers of the bag together using embroidery floss or yarn like you would a blanket, as I did on the blue-and-white bag, or leaving it as is.

MATERIALS

Yardage is based on 42"-wide fabric.

½ yard of fabric for outer-bag background squares, binding, and straps

½ yard *total* of assorted coordinating fabrics for alternate squares and straps

⅜ yards of a different coordinating fabric for lining

½ yard of batting

4 or 8 buttons (depending on your preference), ¾" to 1" diameter

CUTTING

From the fabric for background squares, binding, and straps, cut:
2 strips, 3½" x 42"; crosscut into 20 squares, 3½" x 3½"
2 strips, 1½" x 28"
1 strip, 2" x 30"

From the assorted fabrics for alternate squares and straps, cut a *total* of:
20 squares, 3½" x 3½"

From one of the fabrics for alternate squares and straps, cut:
2 strips, 1½" x 28"

From the lining fabric, cut:
2 rectangles, 12¼" x 15¼"

From the batting, cut:
2 rectangles, 12¼" x 15¼"
2 strips, 1½" x 28"

MAKING THE BAG

Use ¼"-wide seam allowances throughout.

1. Lay out 10 background fabric squares and 10 alternate fabric squares into five rows of four squares each, alternating the two different squares in each row and from row to row. When you are satisfied with the arrangement, sew the squares in each row together. Press the seam allowance of each row in the same direction, pressing in opposite directions from row to row.

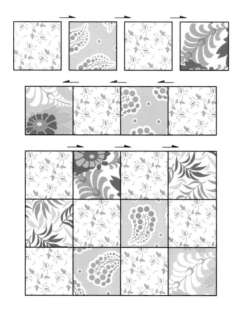

2. Sew the rows together. Because the seam allowances were pressed in opposite directions, they should nest together and line up neatly on the right side. Press the new seam allowances in the same direction.

Nested seams

3. Repeat steps 1 and 2 for the other side of the bag.

4. Place the front and back panels right sides together, matching the seam allowances along the sides. Sew around the side and bottom edges, leaving the top edge open. Clip the bottom corners at an angle, and then turn the piece right side out. This is the outer bag.

5. Layer a batting rectangle on the wrong side of each lining rectangle. With the lining pieces right sides together and using a walking foot, sew around the side and bottom edges like you did for the outer bag. Trim the batting from the seam allowances. Clip the bottom corners as in step 4, but do not turn the piece.

6. Place the lining inside the outer bag, wrong sides together, aligning the side seams and top raw edges. Refer to "Binding" (page 109) to use the 2" x 30" binding strip to bind the top raw edges, making sure the binding seam lines up with one of the side seams.

7. To make the straps, layer two different 1½" x 28" strips right sides together. Place a batting strip on top. Sew around three sides, leaving one short end open. Turn the strip right side out and press. Ladder stitch the end closed. Repeat with the remaining fabric and batting strips to make a second strap.

8. Position the straps on one side of the bag and stitch them down as shown at the point where the buttons will be placed. Sew the buttons over the stitching using matching or invisible thread. Repeat on the other side of the bag.

flea market purse

I don't usually go for old-fashioned floral or country prints, but every once in a while I'm drawn to a particularly feminine and romantic fabric. I also love the wonderful Japanese "country" prints, which are a little different than the folksy country styles common to North American quilt shops. As is befitting soft florals and country scenes, I created a purse that would be at home on a lazy Sunday drive in the family Plymouth, a tea party, or of course a trip to your local flea market.

MATERIALS

Yardage is based on 42"-wide fabric.

½ yard of country print for outer purse

½ yard of small-scale print for lining

½ yard of heavyweight fusible interfacing, such as Pellon Decor-Bond

½"-diameter magnetic clasp

Pair of U-shaped bag handles with small holes to slip tabs through

4" x 6¾" piece of bookboard*

Bookboard is available at paper and art supply stores.

CUTTING

Use the pattern on page 31 and follow the instructions below the pattern to make the purse-body template for cutting the outer-purse, lining, and interfacing pieces.

From the outer-purse fabric, cut:
2 purse-body pieces
1 rectangle, 3" x 5½"
4 squares, 4" x 4"

From the lining fabric, cut:
2 purse-body pieces
1 rectangle, 4½" x 10½"
1 rectangle, 7¾" x 9"
1 rectangle, 3" x 5½"

From the interfacing, cut:
2 purse-body pieces
1 rectangle, 4½" x 5¼"
1 rectangle, 3" x 5½"
2 squares, 2" x 2"

MAKING THE BAG BODY

Use ½"-wide seam allowances throughout unless other-wise indicated.

1. Fold the small-scale print 4½" x 10½" piece in half right sides together to make a 4½" x 5¼" rectangular pocket; press. Follow the manufacturer's instructions to fuse the interfacing 4½" x 5¼" piece to the wrong side of one half.

2. Using a ¼" seam allowance, sew along both long sides and just around the corners of the open short end, leaving most of that edge open. Clip the corners. Turn the pocket right side out, roll the seams to the wrong side (page 106), turn the open edge under ¼", and press.

3. Center the pocket onto a purse-body lining piece 2½" from the upper curved edge, with the folded edge of the pocket facing up. Topstitch a scant ⅛" from the edge around the two sides and bottom of the pocket.

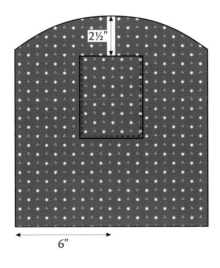

4. With right sides together, sew around the two sides and the bottom of the purse-body lining pieces, leaving a 5" gap in one side seam for turning. Clip the corners and press the seam allowances open.

5. Iron the purse-body interfacing pieces to the wrong sides of the country print purse-body pieces. Center and iron one interfacing 2" x 2" square over the previously adhered interfacing on one country print

purse-body piece ½" from the top of the curved edge. This is where the magnetic clasp will be attached.

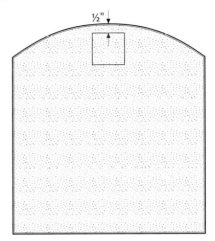

6. With right sides together, sew around the two sides and the bottom of the country print purse-body pieces. Clip the corners and press the seam allowances open. This will be the outer purse.

7. With the wrong sides out, press the bottom corners of the lining and outer purse flat as shown. Measure 2" from each corner and draw a line perpendicular to the seam. Sew along this line on both corners of the lining and outer purse. Trim ½" from the stitching line.

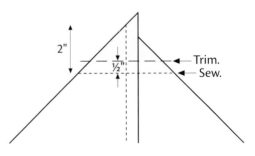

8. Turn the outer purse right side out and press.

9. Put the outer bag inside the lining, right sides together. Make sure the lining pocket side is opposite the outer-purse side where the magnetic clasp will be attached. Align and pin the top raw edges together.

10. Sew all the way around the top edge. Clip the top curves and trim the seam allowance to about ⅛" at the side seams. Turn the bag to the right side through the gap in the lining, roll the top seam (page 106), and press. Stitch the gap in the lining closed.

ADDING THE CLASP, HANDLES, AND INSERT

1. Iron the 3" x 5½" interfacing rectangle to the wrong side of the 3" x 5½" lining rectangle. Iron the remaining 2" x 2" interfacing square to the wrong side of one end of this piece. This will be the end to which the magnetic clasp will be attached.

2. Follow the instructions enclosed with the magnetic clasp to attach the male end through the lining and two layers of interfacing so that the top of the closure is 1" from the end of the tab.

3. With right sides together and using a ¼" seam allowance, sew the lining and outer-purse 3" x 5½" rectangles together around the two long sides and one short side, sewing just around the corners of the remaining short side. Clip the corners, turn the closure tab right side out, and roll the seams (page 106). Turn under the opening ¼", and press.

4. Using matching thread for the outer-purse and lining fabrics, topstitch a scant ⅛" from the edge all the way around the tab.

5. Sew the tab to the outer-purse back, centering it 2¼" from the curved edge.

6. To make the handle tabs, press under ¼" on two opposite sides of a 4" x 4" country print square. Press the piece in half, matching the remaining raw edges. Unfold, turn the raw edges in toward the center crease, refold on the center crease, and press again. Insert the end of the tab through a hole in the handle to be sure it fits. Depending on the size of the tab holes and the weight of your fabric, you may need to adjust the width of the tabs. As shown, the finished width is 1". Once the width is correct, take the strip out of the handle and topstitch around all four sides of the tab a scant ⅛" from the edges, using matching thread. Repeat for the remaining three tabs.

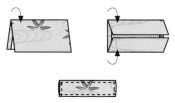

7. Slip a tab through the slots in one handle. On the purse back, position the outer portion of the tab on the outside of the bag. I positioned mine 1¼" from the closure tab and about ¼" below the bottom of the tab; depending on your handle style, you may choose to sew them higher or lower. Stagger the tab ends so the end in front covers the end behind it to reduce bulk. Pin the tabs in place.

8. Pick a top thread and a bottom thread to match the outer-purse and lining fabrics, and then sew down the tabs as show.

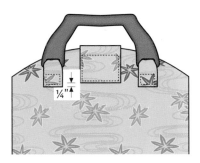

9. Repeat steps 4 and 5 on the purse front with the remaining handle, matching the tab placement so that both handles are at the same level.

10. To attach the female side of the magnetic closure to the front of the bag, first close the bag so the top curved edges meet, and then fold the tab closure over. Mark where the male end of the magnetic clasp touches the front of the bag. Attach the clasp at this point.

11. To create the insert, fold the 7¾" x 9" lining rectangle in half along the long edge, right sides together. Sew around one short and one long edge, using a ¼"-wide seam allowance. Clip the corners and turn the piece right side out.

12. Slide the bookboard into the lining piece from step 11. Turn under the seam allowance at the open end and stitch it closed. Place the insert in the bottom of the purse.

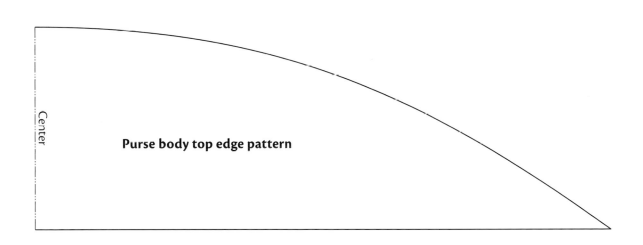

Center

Purse body top edge pattern

Draw an 11" x 12" rectangle on template plastic. Align purse body top edge pattern with 12" side, matching centers and ends. Trace pattern onto template plastic. Flip template plastic over and align pattern with opposite side of rectangle; trace to complete template. Cut out.

tropical vintage patchwork bag

This variation of the Vintage is the New Modern Patchwork Bag (page 25) makes me think of a '50s beauty, in a white sundress, impossibly high heels, and huge, glamorous sunglasses walking down a Miami boardwalk on a brilliantly sunny day. I guess that's what Seattlites daydream about in the middle of a cold, wet winter.

This bag is an example of how some simple changes result in a completely different look. Starting with the basic patchwork idea from the Vintage is the New Modern Patchwork Bag, I eliminated a row of squares and used store-bought handles with handmade tabs.

MATERIALS

Yardage is based on 42"-wide fabric.

½ yard of pink print for outer bag, binding, and handle tabs

½ yard of chartreuse print for lining

¼ yard of blue print for outer bag

½ yard of batting

Pair of U-shaped wooden bag handles with small holes at base to slip tabs through

CUTTING

From the pink print, cut:
2 strips, 3½" x 42"; crosscut into 16 squares, 3½" x 3½"

1 strip, 2" x 30"

4 rectangles, 4" x 6½"

From the blue print, cut:
2 strips, 3½" x 42"; crosscut into 16 squares, 3½" x 3½"

From the chartreuse print, cut:
2 squares, 12½" x 12½"

From the batting, cut:
2 squares, 12½" x 12½"

MAKING THE BAG

Use ¼"-wide seam allowances throughout.

1. Lay out eight pink squares and eight blue squares in four rows of four squares each, alternating the different squares in each row and from row to row. When you are satisfied with the arrangements, sew the squares in each row together. Press the seam allowance of each row in the same direction and press in opposite directions from row to row.

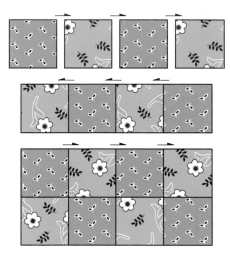

2. Sew the rows together. Because the seam allowances were pressed in opposite directions, they should nest together and line up neatly on the right side. Press the new seam allowances in the same direction.

Nested seams

3. Repeat steps 1 and 2 for the other side of the bag.

4. Place the front and back panels right sides together, matching the seam allowances along the sides. Sew around the side and bottom edges, leaving the top edge open. Clip the bottom corners at an angle, and then turn the piece right side out. This is the outer bag.

5. Layer a piece of batting on the wrong side of each chartreuse lining square. With right sides together and using a walking foot, sew around the side and bottom edges like you did for the outer bag. Trim the batting from the seam allowances. Clip the bottom corners as in step 4, but do not turn the piece.

6. Place the lining inside the outer bag, wrong sides together, aligning the side seams and top raw edges. Refer to "Binding" (page 109) to use the 2" x 30" pink strip to bind the top raw edges, making sure the binding seam lines up with one of the side seams.

7. To make the handle tabs, press under ¼" on both short ends of a pink 4" x 6½" rectangle. Press the piece in half lengthwise, wrong sides together. Unfold, turn the raw edges in toward the center crease, refold on the center crease, and press again. Insert the end of the tab through a hole in the handle to be sure it fits. Depending on the size of the tab holes and the weight of your fabric, you may need to adjust the width of the tabs. As is, the finished width is 1". If the width is correct, take the strip out of the handle and topstitch around all four sides of the tab a scant ⅛" from the edges. Repeat for the remaining three tabs.

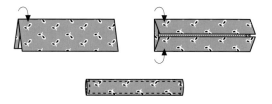

8. Slip the tabs through the handles and even up the ends. Position the handles in a way that looks good to you, and pin the tabs down, making sure both handles are even. (I like to hold the bag by the handles at this point and view it from various angles, making sure my eye-balling is correct.)

9. Using matching thread, sew down the tabs as shown.

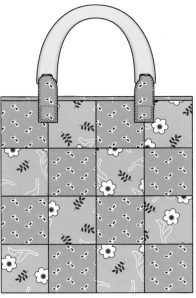

dinner party grocery bag

This is a roomy, versatile tote bag. With its water- and mess-resistant oilcloth lining, it makes a perfect grocery bag, and the version with pockets would make a great diaper bag. It also stands up quite nicely by itself, which all combined makes it a cut above your average brown paper bag or canvas tote. With the securely stitched nylon straps, you can really load it up. If you crave a bit more organization in your carryalls, instructions for including inside pockets follow the basic instructions.

I find regular cotton to be too light-weight for the lining of this bag, and of course it won't hold up very well to spills. But if you have the perfect cotton print for the lining, there is a way to have the best of both worlds. Cut two sets of lining pieces, one set from cotton and one set from clear vinyl. Baste the cotton pieces to the matching vinyl pieces, the right side of the cotton against the vinyl, and treat these units as single lining pieces. Your finished bag will be lined with clear vinyl, but the cotton print will show through.

MATERIALS

Yardage is based on 42"-wide fabric.

⅞ yard of home-decor or canvas fabric for outer bag

⅞ yard of coordinating oilcloth or vinyl-coated fabric for lining

2⅝ yards of 1"- or 2"-wide nylon or cotton webbing

6¾" x 11¾" piece of bookboard or plywood* (no thicker than ³⁄₁₆")

Bookboard is available at paper and art supply stores. Use a large X-Acto knife or mat knife on an old cutting mat to cut bookboard and a hand- or powersaw to cut the plywood.

CUTTING

From the outer-bag fabric, cut:
2 rectangles, 13" x 14"
2 rectangles, 8" x 14"
1 rectangle, 8" x 13"

From the lining fabric, cut:
2 rectangles, 13" x 14"
2 rectangles, 8" x 14"
1 rectangle, 8" x 13"
1 rectangle, 12¾" x 14½"

MAKING THE BAG

Use ½"-wide seam allowances throughout unless otherwise indicated.

1. Cut the webbing in half crosswise to make two equal lengths.

2. On the right side of a canvas 13" x 14" rectangle, make marks 2½" in from both bottom corners. With the raw edges aligned along the bottom edge and the outside edge aligned with the marks, pin one webbing length to the fabric so it forms a loop at the top. Repeat with the remaining webbing piece and 13" x 14" rectangle.

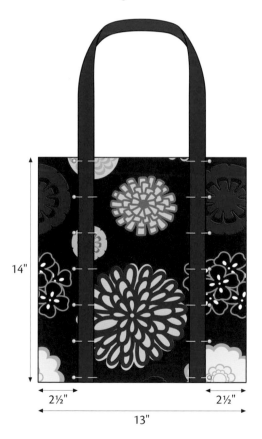

3. Using matching thread, sew the straps in place along the outer and inner edges, stopping 1" from the top of the rectangles and backstitching at the beginning and end.

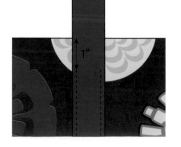

4. With right sides together, sew the canvas 8" x 14" rectangles to each long edge of one strap rectangle from step 3, ending ½" before the bottom raw edge. Add the remaining strap rectangle to the end of this unit, and then join the ends to create a tube, again stopping ½" before the bottom edge. Turn wrong side out and press the seam allowances open.

5. With right sides together, pin the canvas 8" x 13" piece to the bottom edges of the tube you've created. Fold the corners up 90° so that the bag sits flat.

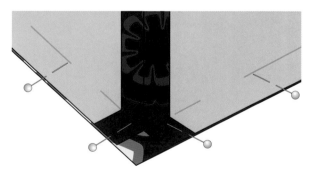

6. Starting in the middle of a long side, stitch around the bottom. At each corner, take two or three extra stitches across the pivot point. Turn the outer bag right side out.

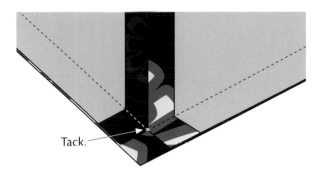

Tack.

7. Repeat steps 4 and 5 with the lining 13" x 14" rectangles and 8" x 14" rectangles, leaving an 8" gap along one long edge for turning. You will eventually pull the entire bag through this hole, so make sure to backstitch before and after the gap for extra strength. Repeat step 6 to add the 8" x 13" rectangle for the lining bottom, but do not turn the bag to the right side. When pinning oilcloth or vinyl-coated fabric, pin within the seam allowances so the resulting holes won't show.

8. With right sides together, place the outer bag inside the lining bag, sandwiching the straps between the layers and making sure they aren't in the seam allowance. Align the top raw edges and "pin" them together—I recommend metal hair clips for this seam, except around the corners where pins are helpful in matching the corner seams more accurately. Stitch all around the top edge.

9. Turn the bag by pulling it through the gap you left in the lining. Whipstitch the gap closed.

10. Roll the seam along the top edge (page 106) as well as you can and use clips to secure it. You'll find that rolling the seams isn't as easy with oilcloth, but with some fussing you can get the seam quite neat. Using matching thread, topstitch ½" all around the top of the bag, backstitching over the handles.

11. To create the insert, fold the lining 12¾" x 14½" rectangle in half, right sides together, to make a piece that is 12¾" x 7⅜". Sew around one short and the long raw edge using a ¼"-wide seam allowance. Clip the corners and turn the piece right side out.

12. Slide the book board into the lining piece from step 11, pushing it all the way to the end. Turn under the seam allowance of the opening and whipstitch it closed. Place the insert in the bottom of the bag. It should fit snugly, but if you want a more secure hold, adhere a few pieces of self-adhesive Velcro to the insert and the bag bottom.

VARIATION: ADDING INSIDE POCKETS

Adding pockets to the inside perimeter of the bag before you sew the bag pieces together is really easy, and you'll only need an additional ½ yard of your lining fabric. You can also sew the pockets to the outside of the bag if you prefer. The pockets will add bulk to all but your top seam, however, so you might try a version without pockets first to get the hang of sewing on the bottom panel.

In addition to the pieces you've already cut (page 37), from the lining fabric, cut:

2 rectangles, 13" x 17"

2 rectangles, 8" x 17"

1. Fold each pocket piece in half along the long edges, wrong sides together, to make pieces 8½" tall.

2. Using matching thread, topstitch ¼" from the fold of each pocket piece.

3. Layer the pocket pieces on the right sides of each lining piece, excluding the bottom. Match the bottom raw edges.

4. Follow the instructions for making the bag, adding the pockets in the side and bottom seams. Don't forget to leave an 8" gap in the lining so you can turn the bag.

bird-watcher messenger bag

I'm pretty practical when it comes to most accessories, and I wanted an everyday bag that was easy to carry, had enough room for my daily essentials, and could keep those essentials organized—unlike my previous "black hole" bag. Enter the Bird-Watcher, a perfect union of purse and messenger bag. It's not as large as a true messenger bag, but it has the same combination of useful pockets, a flat, low-profile design, and a nice long strap you can wear across your chest. A cell-phone pocket on the side guarantees no digging around when you're ringing, and the front two pockets are just the right size for an MP3 player, smartphone, or small spiral notebook.

MATERIALS

Yardage is based on 42"-wide fabric unless otherwise indicated. The outer-bag and lining fabrics used in the sample are directional. If your fabric isn't directional, you may need less yardage of those fabrics.

⅞ yard of pink wood-grain print for lining, strap, and top clip tab

¾ yard of olive bird print for outer bag, strap, bottom clip tab, and cell phone pocket C

⅜ yard or fat quarter of olive circle print for front pocket A

⅜ yard or fat quarter of olive striped fabric for front pocket B and cell phone pocket C lining

1⅛ yards of 22"-wide mediumweight fusible interfacing

¼ yard of heavyweight fusible interfacing, such as Pellon Decor-Bond

¾"-wide contoured plastic quick-release clip

CUTTING

Follow the illustrated cutting guides for the outer-bag, lining, and interfacing pieces to make the best use of your yardage. This project has a lot of pieces, so you may want to label them as you cut them.

From the olive bird print, cut:

2 rectangles, 10" x 11" (front and back outer panels)

2 rectangles, 4" x 11" (side panels)

1 rectangle, 10" x 11½" (flap)

2 strips, 3" x 26½" (strap)

1 rectangle, 4" x 10" (bottom)

1 rectangle, 4" x 6" (pocket C)

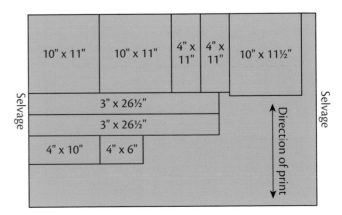

Olive bird print cutting guide

From the pink wood-grain print, cut:

2 strips, 3" x 26½" (strap lining)

2 rectangles, 10" x 11" (front and back lining)

2 rectangles, 4" x 11" (side lining)

1 rectangle, 10" x 11½" (flap lining)

1 rectangle, 3 x 6½" (top clip tab)

1 rectangle, 4" x 10" (bottom lining)

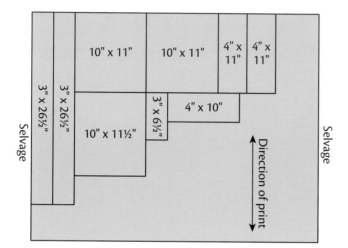

Pink wood-grain print cutting guide

From the olive striped fabric, cut:

1 rectangle, 10" x 15" (pocket B)

1 rectangle, 4" x 6" (pocket C lining)

From the olive circle print, cut:

1 rectangle, 10" x 11" (pocket A)

1 rectangle, 3" x 6½" (bottom clip tab)

From the mediumweight interfacing, cut:

2 rectangles, 10" x 11" (front and back panels)

2 rectangles, 4" x 11" (side panels)

1 rectangle, 4" x 10" (bottom)

1 rectangle, 4" x 6" (pocket C)

1 rectangle, 10" x 11½" (flap)

1 rectangle, 7½" x 10" (pocket B)

1 rectangle, 5½" x 10" (pocket A)

Mediumweight interfacing cutting guide

From the heavyweight interfacing, cut:

2 strips, 3" x 26"

MAKING THE OUTER BAG AND LINING

Use ½"-wide seam allowances throughout unless otherwise indicated.

1. Follow the manufacturer's instructions to fuse the corresponding-sized mediumweight interfacing pieces to the wrong side of the bird print front, back, side, bottom, and flap pieces.

2. Pin the bird print and pink wood-grain print flap pieces right sides together. Sew around two long sides and one short side. Clip the corners, turn right side out, and press. If you've fussy-cut your flap fabric or if it's directional, take care to sew the correct three sides; the end you sew closed will point down.

3. Prepare the clip tabs. Press under ¼" on the short ends of the top and bottom clip-tab pieces. Press the strips in half lengthwise, wrong sides together. Unfold, turn the long edges in toward the center crease, refold on the center crease, and press again. Topstitch around all four sides of each tab piece.

4. With right sides out, fold pocket piece A in half to make a 10" x 5½" piece. Open up the piece and fuse the corresponding interfacing piece to the wrong side of one half, and then refold the piece. Using matching thread, topstitch ⅛" from the fold of the pocket. Repeat with the pocket B fabric and interfacing pieces to make a 10" x 7½" piece.

5. To make the cell phone pocket (pocket C, which is on the side of the bag), fuse the interfacing rectangle for pocket C to the wrong side of the appropriate bird print rectangle. With right sides together, sew the bird print and olive striped cell phone rectangles together along one short edge. Press the seam allowance open and fold the joined pieces in half along the seam line, wrong sides together. Topstitch ⅛" from the fold.

6. Layer front pocket A on front pocket B, matching the bottom raw edges. Measure in 5" from one side and draw a line up the center of pocket A using the marking tool of your choice. Pin the pieces together and stitch on the marked line. Place the pocket panel on the right side of the front panel, matching the bottom raw edges; pin in place.

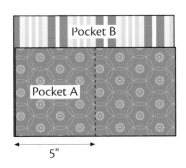

7. Decide on which side of the bag you would like the cell phone pocket C. I wear my bag so it hangs on my right side, so I would place the pocket on the right side panel of the bag so it faces "front" when I'm carrying the bag. If you plan to hang the bag on your left side, consider sewing the pocket to the left side of the bag. With right sides together, stitch the side panels (including the pocket C piece) to

the sides of the front panel (including the pocket A/B piece), stopping ½" from the bottom edges. Add the back panel to one side of this unit, and then join the opposite side panel to the back panel to create a tube, again stopping ½" before the bottom edge. Press the seam allowances open.

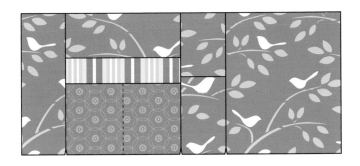

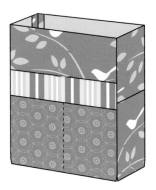

8. Pin the olive circle print front clip tab to the front panel over the stitching line, aligning one end with the bottom raw edge. Turn the tube wrong side out.

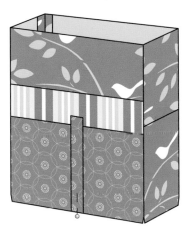

9. With right sides together, pin the bird print bottom piece to the bottom edges of the tube you've created. Fold the corners up 90° so that the bag sits flat.

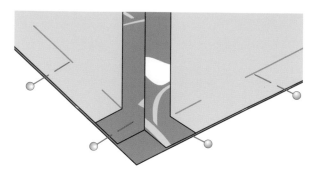

10. Starting in the middle of a long side, stitch around the bottom. At each corner, take two or three extra stitches across the pivot point. Turn the outer bag right side out.

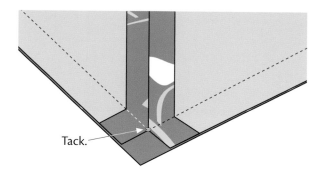

Tack.

11. To make the lining, sew the pink wood-grain print front, side, back, and bottom panels together in the same manner as you did for the outer bag, leaving a 6" gap in the center of one side seam. Do not turn the lining to the right side.

COMPLETING THE BAG

1. Place the outer bag inside the lining bag, right sides together.

2. With the lining pieces facing each other, insert the flap piece between the lining back and outer-bag back, with the top raw edges and corner seams aligned. Pin through all the layers.

3. Sew around the entire top of the bag, backstitching over the corner seams for added strength. Pull the bag through the gap in the lining seam. Whipstitch the gap closed.

4. To make the strap, sew the bird print strap strips together end to end, using a ¼"-wide seam allowance, to make a piece 52½" long. Repeat with the pink wood-grain print strips. Fuse the heavyweight interfacing strips to the wrong side of one of the pieced strips, butting the ends together at the center of the strip and leaving ¼" of the fabric strip uncovered at each end. Layer the fabric strips right sides together.

5. Using a ½"-wide seam allowance, sew around two long sides and one end. Clip the corners and turn the strap right side out. Once the strap is turned, roll the seams (page 106) toward the lining and press. Turn under the raw edges on the open end ¼" and press. Topstitch ⅛" from the edge around the entire perimeter of the strap.

6. Position the ends of the straps 3" from the top of the bag on each side panel. Stitch the ends down as shown.

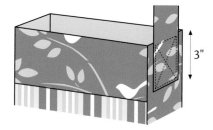

3"

7. Thread the top clip tab—made from the pink wood-grain fabric—through the female half of the clip. Slightly stagger the ends so the longest side is on top. Center and pin the tab to the lining side of the flap about 4¾" from the top edge. Pick a top thread and a bottom thread to match the lining and outer-flap fabrics, and then sew the tab down as shown.

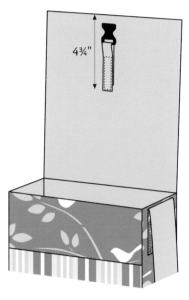

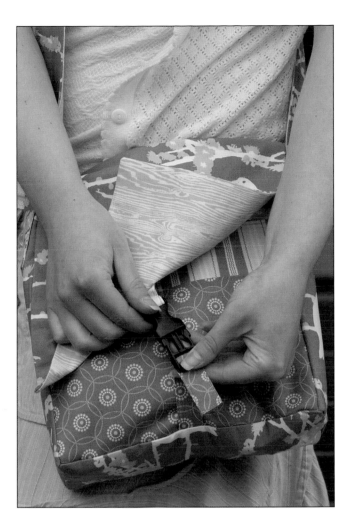

8. Thread the male half of the clip through the bottom clip tab.

cases, covers,

and zippered bags

zippered kit bag

This basic zippered case is great for all kinds of small items (and it's the perfect size for tampons). Once you see how it's constructed, making bags in any size you want will be a snap. Make a matched set in different sizes, add a hand-made zipper pull, or machine appliqué a design to the outer fabric before you sew the bag together. Use batting instead of interfacing, or in addition to, to give a bit of body to the bag.

And speaking of interfacing, though I ask for it here it's entirely optional. If you'll be keeping sharp items in the bag, like tweezers or a set of keys, interfacing will help protect the bag against tears or holes. If you prefer a "softer" bag, simply leave out the interfacing and skip step 1.

This little bag is a natural choice for makeup or travel-sized toiletries. Use oilcloth for the lining, skip the interfacing, and your bag will be fortified against leaks.

MATERIALS

Yardage is based on 42"-wide fabric, unless otherwise indicated.

¼ yard of yellow print for outer bag

¼ yard of green print for lining

¼ yard of 22"-wide mediumweight fusible interfacing

7" zipper to match outer fabric

CUTTING

From *each* of the outer-bag fabric, lining fabric, and interfacing, cut:

2 rectangles, 6" x 8"

MAKING THE BAG

Use ½"-wide seam allowances throughout.

1. Follow the manufacturer's instructions to fuse the interfacing to the wrong side of each lining rectangle.

2. Place a lining piece on your work surface, right side up, with the long edges at the top and bottom. With the zipper closed and right side up, place the zipper at the top of the lining piece, aligning the top edges. Place an outer-bag rectangle, wrong side up, over the zipper and lining, aligning the top edges. Pin the layers together along the top edge.

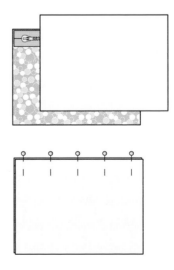

3. Using a zipper foot, sew along the top edge of the zipper, as close to the teeth as possible, backstitching at the beginning and end. Press the outer-bag and lining rectangles up and away from the zipper (gently pulling the fabric away from the zipper while using the point of your iron works well here).

4. Repeat steps 2 and 3 with the remaining outer-bag and lining rectangles on the opposite side of the zipper, making sure the rectangle sides are aligned with the previous half.

5. Using a zipper foot, topstitch a scant ⅛" from the seam on both sides of the zipper, backstitching at the beginning and end. If you like, choose a top thread to match the outer fabric and a bobbin thread to match the lining fabric.

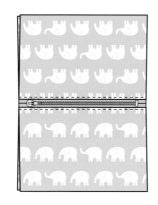

6. Unzip the zipper halfway. You will be turning the bag inside out through the open zipper, so you don't want to forget this step!

7. Bring the outer-bag rectangles right sides together; pin along the raw edges. Repeat with the lining rectangles. Make sure the zipper is folded evenly at both ends.

8. Sew around the perimeter of the entire piece, leaving a 3" gap along the bottom edge of the lining. Go very slowly over the zipper tape at each end, stopping and using the hand wheel for a few stitches to make sure you don't sew over any zipper teeth. After sewing around the entire perimeter, carefully go over the zipper areas one more time for added strength. Trim around the zipper area close to the seam allowance and clip your corners.

9. Pull the outer bag through the lining gap and open zipper. Stitch the gap in the lining closed, and then turn the bag to the right side. Push the lining into the bag.

10. Press your new bag, fill it with this and that, and you're done!

evening essentials wristlet

A variation of the Zippered Kit Bag, this wristlet is what you turn to when you don't want to be weighed down by a handbag. It's perfect for a night of dancing or anytime you only need to carry the basics.

MATERIALS

Yardage is based on 42"-wide fabric unless otherwise indicated.

¼ yard or scrap of a black-and-white large-scale floral print for outer bag and strap

¼ yard or scrap of teal print for lining

¼ yard or scrap of 22"-wide mediumweight fusible interfacing

5"-long zipper*

*This length may be hard to find in the color you want. You can purchase a longer zipper and follow the instructions in the tip box (page 53) to shorten it.

CUTTING

From the outer-bag and strap fabric, cut:

2 rectangles, 5" x 6"

1 strip, 3" x 12"

From both the lining fabric and interfacing, cut:

2 rectangles, 5" x 6"

MAKING THE WRISTLET

Use ½"-wide seam allowances throughout.

1. Follow the manufacturer's instructions to fuse the interfacing to the wrong side of each lining piece.

2. Place a lining piece on your work surface, right side up, with the long edges at the top and bottom. With the zipper closed and right side up, place the zipper at the top of the lining piece, aligning the top edges. Place an outer-bag rectangle, wrong side up, over the zipper and lining, aligning the top edges. Pin the layers together along the top edge.

3. Using a zipper foot, sew along the top edge of the zipper, as close to the teeth as possible, backstitching at the beginning and end. Press the outer-bag and lining rectangles up and away from the zipper (gently pulling the fabric away from the zipper while using the point of your iron works well here).

4. Repeat steps 2 and 3 with the remaining outer-bag and lining rectangles on the opposite side of the zipper, making sure the rectangle sides are aligned with the previous half.

5. Using a zipper foot, topstitch a scant ⅛" from the seam on both sides of the zipper, backstitching at the beginning and end. If you like, choose a top thread to match the outer fabric and a bobbin thread to match the lining fabric.

6. Prepare the strap. Press the 3" x 12" strip in half lengthwise, wrong sides together. Unfold, turn the raw edges of the strip in to the center crease, refold on the center crease, and press again. Unfold and turn the new edges into the center crease, fold everything in half along this crease, and press one last time. Using matching thread and a scant ⅛" seam, sew along the open edge of the strap from end to end.

7. Unzip the zipper halfway. You will be turning the bag inside out through the open zipper, so you don't want to forget this step!

8. Position the strap on the right side of one outer-bag piece about ½" below the zipper tab, matching raw edges.

9. Bring the outer-bag rectangles right sides together; pin along the raw edges. Repeat with the lining rectangles. Make sure the zipper is folded evenly at both ends.

10. Sew around the perimeter of the entire piece, leaving a 3" gap along the bottom edge of the lining. Go very slowly over the zipper tape at each end, stopping and using the hand wheel for a few stitches to make sure you don't sew over any zipper teeth. After sewing around the entire perimeter, carefully go over the zipper areas one more time

for added strength. Trim around the zipper area close to the seam allowance.

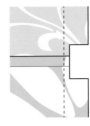

11. Clip the corners and pull the outer bag through the lining gap and open zipper. Stitch the gap in the lining closed, and then push the lining into the bag. Press your new bag.

ZIP TIP

To shorten a longer zipper to the correct length, make sure the zipper is closed, and then measure from the bottom of the tab to the length needed. Hand or machine bartack across the teeth at that point several times. Cut away the excess zipper tape ¾" to 1" below the bar tack, and then carefully trim out the zipper teeth in the excess.

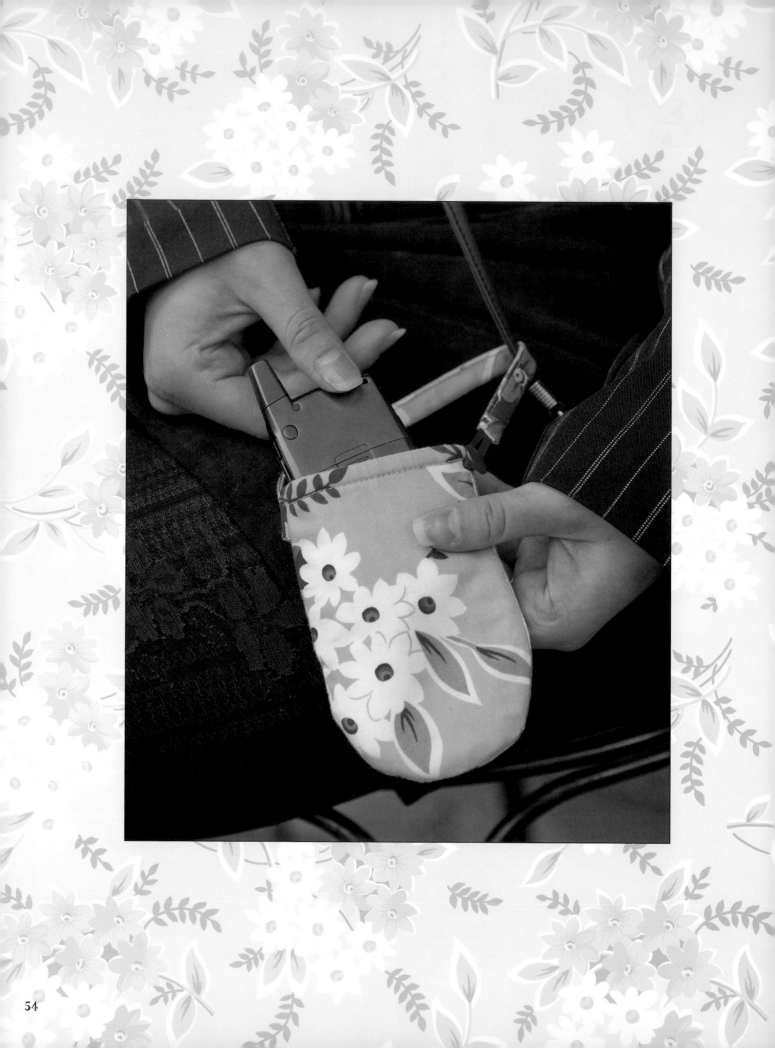

cell phone case

This is a simple little case to clip to the inside of your bag so your cell phone is close at hand. No more digging around at the bottom of a stuffed bag while everyone in the library glares at you! This is an easy project, but its diminutive size means you just have to take a bit more care sewing the small pieces together.

MATERIALS

Scrap of blue floral for the outer case and strap

Scrap of red print for lining

Scrap of batting

Coordinating button and scrap of ribbon or thin cord

CUTTING

Use the patterns on page 57 to make the templates for cutting the outer-case, lining, and batting pieces.

From the outer-case and strap fabric, cut:
2 outer-case pieces
1 strip, 1½" x 8"

From *each* of the lining fabric and batting, cut:
2 lining and batting pieces

MAKING THE CASE BODY

Use ¼"-wide seam allowances throughout.

1. With right sides together, sew the outer-case pieces together around three sides, leaving the straight top edge open. Clip the seam allowance along the curve. Turn the piece right side out.

2. Layer a batting piece on the wrong side of each lining piece. Place the lining pieces right sides together. Using a walking foot, sew around the side and bottom edges, leaving a 2" gap along one long side. Trim the batting from the seam allowance. Clip the seam allowance along the curve, but do not turn the piece to the right side.

3. Place the outer case inside the lining and match the top raw edges. Sew all the way around the top of the case.

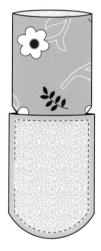

4. Turn the case to the right side through the gap in the lining. Roll the top seam (page 106) toward the lining and press the case.

5. Topstitch ¼" from the top edge.

MAKING AND ADDING THE STRAP

1. Fold under the ends of the 1½" x 8" strip ¼" and press.

2. Press the strip in half lengthwise, wrong sides together. Unfold, turn the raw edges of the strip in to the center crease, refold on the center crease, and then press the strip. Open up the piece, turn the folded edges in to the center crease, refold on the center crease, and iron one last time.

3. To make the loop for the end of the strap, loop the ribbon or cording around the button. Make sure the loop will fit over the button, but that it won't be so big that it will just fall off. Pin the loop between the folds on one end of the strap piece.

4. Topstitch very close to the edge around all three open sides of the strap piece.

5. Stitch the end of the strap without the loop to one of the case side seams as shown.

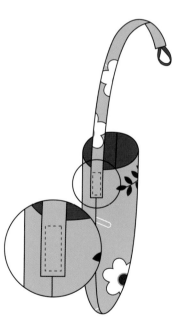

6. Sew the button to the opposite side seam, about ¼" from the top edge.

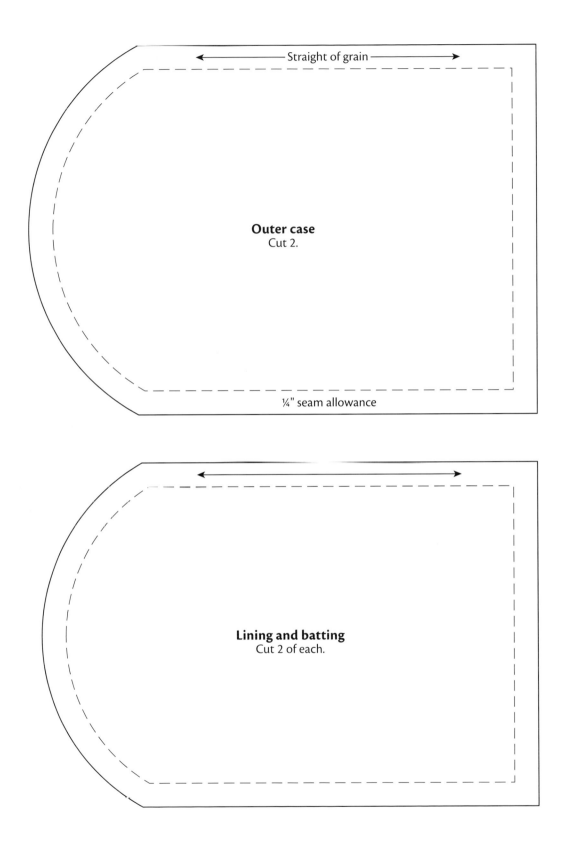

Outer case
Cut 2.

Straight of grain

¼" seam allowance

Lining and batting
Cut 2 of each.

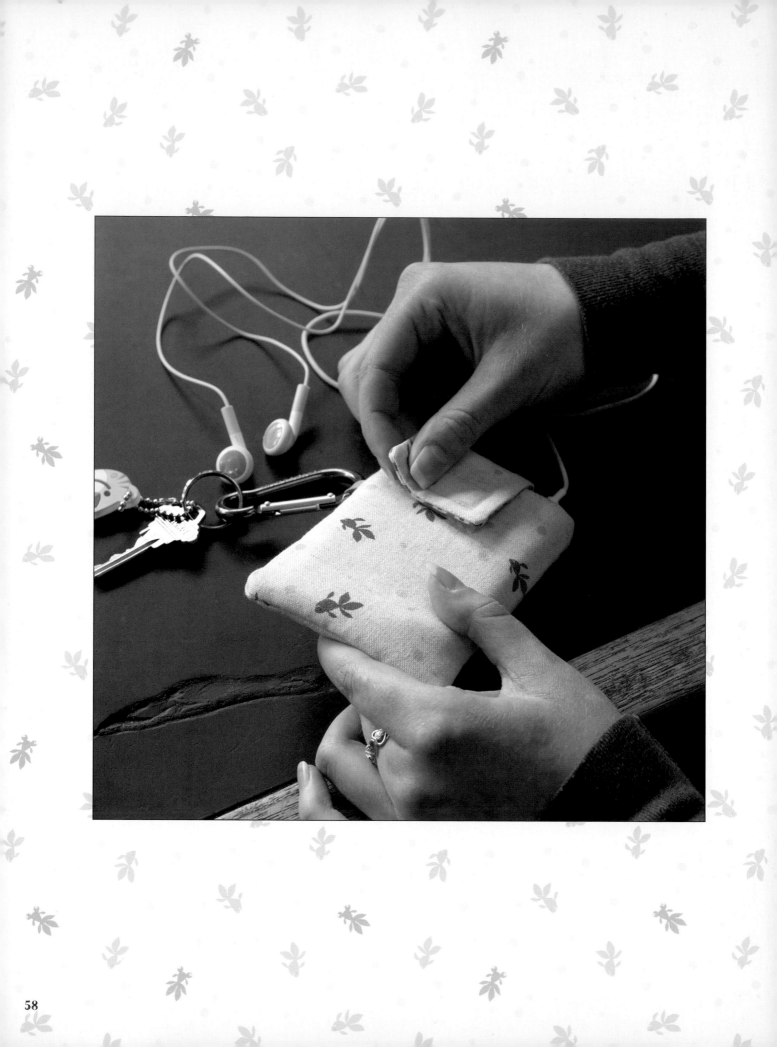

portable media player case

I remember when spending $50 on a portable CD player was a really big deal. I never would have guessed one day I'd be carrying around a media player worth hundreds of dollars, never mind the music itself. With that kind of investment, the least you can do for your media player is protect it with a functional and stylish case.

While a soft cotton fabric is perfect against the scratch-prone surface of music players or smartphones, feel free to try other materials such as flannel or microfleece. I recommend you stay away from anything that may shed excess fibers, however. The ribbon loop for a carabiner or key ring is a handy and simple addition that allows you to attach your case to a bag or attach a key to the case, but it's entirely optional and can simply be omitted. For the paranoid (which includes myself), I'd recommend clipping the player to the inside, not outside, of your bag or purse.

Like the Cell Phone Case, the only thing tricky about this bag is its size—sewing that top seam involves some maneuvering, and there's a bit of hand sewing at the end.

MATERIALS

Yardage is based on 42"-wide fabric.

¼ yard or scraps of goldfish print for outer case

¼ yard or scraps of blue print for lining

Scraps of batting

1½" of ¾"-wide Velcro

1" of ¼"-wide grosgrain ribbon or cording (optional)

Key ring or carabiner clip (optional)

CUTTING

From *each* of the outer-case fabric, lining fabric, and batting, cut:

2 rectangles, 4" x 5¼"

1 rectangle, 2½" x 3¼"

MAKING THE CASE

Use ¼"-wide seam allowances unless otherwise indicated.

1. Use the 2½" x 3¼" rectangles to make the closure. Layer the lining and outer-case rectangles right sides together. Place the batting rectangle on the bottom and pin. Using a walking foot if possible, sew around the two long sides and one short side, leaving one short side open. Clip the corners, turn right side out, roll the seams (page 106), and press.

2. Center and sew the hook portion of the Velcro to the lining on the sewn end of the closure. Make sure the bottom thread matches the outer-case fabric.

3. Layer the outer-case 4" x 5¼" rectangles right sides together. Place the batting rectangles on the top and bottom of the layered outer-case rectangles. If you are adding the ribbon loop for attaching a key ring or carabiner, fold the ribbon in half and sandwich it between the outer-case rectangles, matching the raw edges and positioning it about 1½" from the top edge. The loop should be big enough for whichever clip method you are using (a carabiner will require a slighly larger loop than a key ring).

4. Using a walking foot if possible, stitch around the side and bottom edges, leaving the top edge open. Backstitch over the ribbon for extra strength. Clip the corners, turn right side out, and press.

5. With right sides together, stitch the lining 4" x 5¼" rectangles together along the side and bottom edges, leaving a 3" gap in the middle of one long side. Clip the corners, but do not turn the piece.

6. Place the outer case inside the lining. Position the closure between the two pieces as shown, matching all top raw edges. Make sure the lining side of the closure is against the lining of the outer case.

7. Sew all around the top edge, backstitching over the closure as well as the side seams. Pull the case through the gap in the lining, and then stitch the gap closed. Roll the top seam (page 106) toward the lining and press.

8. Hand stitch the loop portion of the Velcro to the corresponding location on the body of the case, about ¾" from the top edge.

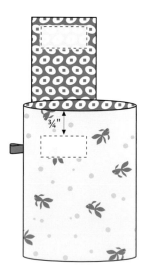

plein air sketchbook cover

This is a great way to dress up a sketchbook or journal. Once you learn the construction, you can make custom-sized covers for just about any kind of book. This cover would make a great canvas for appliqué. It fits snugly, so be careful to roll your seams as much as possible and keep the topstitching close to the edge.

The instructions here are for covering a common-sized sketchbook that is 8⅝" x 5¾". At the end of the instructions, I explain how to measure your own book, should it be a different size.

MATERIALS

Yardage is based on 42"-wide fabric unless otherwise indicated.

⅜ yard of fabric for outer cover

⅜ yard of coordinating fabric for lining

⅜ yard of 22"-wide mediumweight fusible interfacing

CUTTING

From *each* of the outer-cover fabric, lining fabric, and interfacing, cut:
1 rectangle, 10¼" x 21¾"

MAKING THE COVER

Use ½"-wide seam allowances throughout.

1. Follow the manufacturer's instructions to fuse the interfacing rectangle to the wrong side of the lining rectangle.

2. With right sides together, sew the lining and outer-cover rectangles together around all the edges, leaving a 3" gap in the center of the bottom seam.

3. Clip the corners, turn right side out, roll the seams toward the lining (page 106), and press. There's no need to sew the gap closed.

4. Center the spine of the book on the cover. Fold both ends of the cover around the front and back covers of the book (make sure the book will close all the way!). Place a pin at the top and bottom of the cover to mark where the inner edge of the flap ends.

5. Remove the book. Readjust each flap by moving the pin a little over ⅛" toward the short side of the cover. This will create a bit more ease to account for the topstitching in the next step. Refold the flaps and pin them down securely, using the pin as a guide.

6. Starting at the center of the bottom edge, stitch a scant ⅛" all the way around the cover, sewing down the flaps. (In this particular case, use as narrow a seam allowance as you can, more like ¹⁄₁₆" if possible.) Sew around the entire perimeter of the cover, including over the gap at the bottom. Go slowly over the flap corners; there's a lot of bulk at this point. Once you've sewn all the way around, you're ready to pop the book into its new jacket.

CUSTOM-SIZED COVERS

1. To determine the width to cut your fabric and interfacing pieces, measure the height of your book. To this measurement add 1" for seam allowances, plus ¼" for ease and ¼" for topstitching allowance (1½" total).

2. To determine the length to cut your fabric and interfacing pieces, use a flexible tape measure to measure around the book. Start on the inside cover at the point where you'd like your cover flap to extend, measure around the edge of the front cover, around the spine, around the back cover, and over the back flap, ending at the same point on the inside back cover as the inside front cover. To this measurement add 1" for seam allowances and ¼" for topstitching allowance (1¼" total).

3. Use the measurements to cut your fabric and interfacing pieces, and then follow the instructions (at left) to make the cover.

novella composition-book cover

Designed for those ubiquitous composition books (remember the marbled covers?), this fabric cover will help you organize not just your thoughts, but also your pens, pencils, business cards, receipts, fabric swatches, or bus tickets as well. Whether you're penning the first draft of a groundbreaking novel or planning world domination, everything you need will be kept together in style, cleverly disguised and organized.

It looks like a lot of steps, but as with a seemingly complex recipe, once you've prepared the key components, the cover comes together like magic.

MATERIALS

Yardage is based on 42"-wide fabric.

⅜ yard of green tree print for outer cover

½ yard of blue print for lining

⅓ yard of pink print for pencil pocket and pocket-unit lining

¼ yard of purple print for business card pocket

Scrap of brown print for pencil-pocket background

Light- to mediumweight fusible interfacing

14" of coordinating double-faced satin ribbon

CUTTING

There are two different sizes of so-called "standard" marbled composition books. To account for both, I've listed two sets of measurements. If your book is 10¼" x 8", use the first set of measurements. If your book is 9¾" x 7½", use the second set, shown in brackets. It's a small enough difference that the yardage requirements are the same.

From _both_ the green tree print and blue print fabrics, cut:

1 rectangle, 11¾" x 32" [11¼" x 30"]

From the pink print fabric, cut:

1 rectangle, 7" x 8" [7" x 7½"] (pocket-unit lining)

1 rectangle, 4" x 9" [3½" x 9"] (pocket piece B)

From the purple print fabric, cut:

1 rectangle, 5" x 16" [5" x 16"] (pocket piece C)

From the brown print fabric, cut:

1 rectangle, 4" x 7" [3½" x 7"] (pocket piece A)

From the interfacing, cut:

1 rectangle, 11¾" x 32 [11¼" x 30"]

1 rectangle, 7" x 8" [7" x 7½"]

1 rectangle, 4" x 7" [3½" x 7"]

1 rectangle, 4" x 9" [3½" x 9"]

1 rectangle, 5" x 16" [5" x 16"]

MAKING THE MAIN-COVER UNIT

Use ½"-wide seam allowances throughout.

1. Follow the manufacturer's instructions to fuse the corresponding piece of interfacing to the wrong side of the blue print rectangle.

2. Fold the outer-cover rectangle in half widthwise, right sides together, to mark the center. Align one end of the ribbon at the top edge, 1" to the left of the center mark; pin it in place.

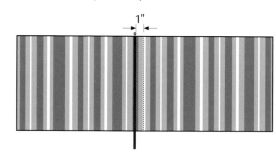

3. With right sides together, pin the outer-cover and lining rectangles together, sandwiching the ribbon between the layers.

4. Stitch all the way around the rectangle, leaving a 4" gap in the center of the bottom edge. Clip the corners, turn right side out, and press. There's no need to sew the gap closed.

5. With the lining side up, topstitch a scant ⅛" along the right edge only.

MAKING THE POCKET UNIT

1. Fuse the remaining interfacing pieces to the wrong side of the corresponding fabric pieces.

2. Press pocket piece B in half across the width of the piece, wrong sides together.

3. Pin piece B to pocket piece A, matching the bottom raw edges. You can leave this pocket as is or divide it into sections for pens and pencils. To divide the pocket, topstitch through all the layers, from the fold of piece B to the bottom raw edges. If you are covering the larger notebook, divide the pocket into three sections as shown; divide the pocket in half for the smaller-sized cover.

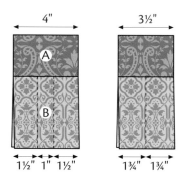

4. Press pocket piece C as shown to make pleats. Topstitch a scant ⅛" from the horizontal folded edges, if desired (just be careful not to stitch through the layer under the fold). Trim ⅛" off the top raw edge.

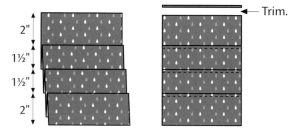

5. With right sides together, lay pocket C over pocket A/B, matching the top raw edges. The bottom edge of piece C will be ⅛" from the bottom raw edge of A/B; this ensures that the fold that forms the bottom pocket will not be sewn into the main seam. Using a ½" seam allowance, sew the center seam as shown. Use lots of steam to press the snot

out of this seam allowance, pressing it open.

6. Place the pocket unit and pocket unit lining pieces right sides together. Sew all the way around the pieces, leaving a 2½" gap 1" from the bottom corner along the pencil pocket edge. Clip the corners, turn to the right side, and press. There is no need to sew the gap closed.

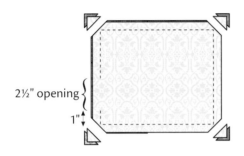

2½" opening

1"

PUTTING IT ALL TOGETHER

1. With the main cover unit and pocket unit right sides up, match the right edges, bottom corners, and bottom edge; pin the pocket in place. Topstitch a scant ⅛" from the *right edge only* the entire length of the pocket.

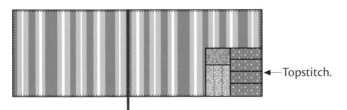

←—Topstitch.

2. Turn the cover over so the lining is faceup and the pocket unit is on the left. Bring the left side of the cover to the lining side so that the entire pocket unit is visible; press.

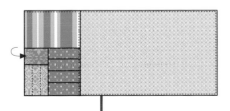

3. Fold the cover around your notebook, folding both ends around the front and back covers. The front cover will already have the fold pressed; use a pin to mark the back cover position and put the notebook aside. Because the width of the inside front cover is determined by the finished width of your pocket piece—and with all those seams things might have shifted—the two ends may not match exactly when you look at the cover from the top, but this doesn't matter. A good fit is more important.

4. Before pressing the right-hand fold, move the edge ¼" from the pin as shown. Press the fold. Pin down both flaps.

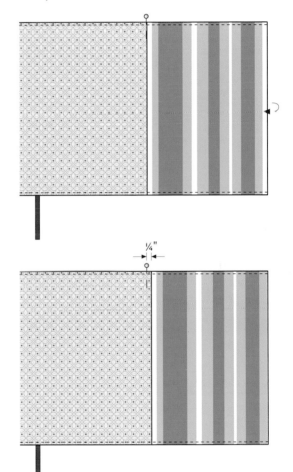

¼"

5. Starting at the center bottom, topstitch around the entire perimeter of the cover a scant ⅛" from the edges. Where the main cover lining meets the pocket piece, I recommend stitching carefully and backstitching, as there's quite a difference in thickness. Backstitch when you reach the beginning, and you're done.

picasso pencil case

Constructed in a similar manner to the Zippered Kit Bag, this pencil case has a slightly wider bottom and an elongated shape to accommodate writing and drawing tools. This would also work great for makeup, especially makeup brushes. For messy items such as charcoal pencils, use oilcloth for the lining and skip the interfacing.

MATERIALS

Yardage is based on 42"-wide fabric.

¼ yard of large-scale print for outer case

¼ yard of small-scale print for lining

¼ yard of 22"-wide mediumweight interfacing

9"-long zipper

CUTTING

Use the pattern on page 69 to make the template for cutting the pieces.

From *each* of the outer-case fabric, lining fabric, and interfacing, cut:
2 pencil case pieces

MAKING THE CASE

Use ½"-wide seam allowances throughout.

1. Follow the manufacturer's instructions to fuse the interfacing to the wrong side of each lining piece.

2. Place a lining piece on your work surface, right side up, with the shortest straight edge at the top. With the zipper closed and right side up, place the zipper at the top of the lining piece, aligning the top edges. Place the shortest straight edge of an outer-bag piece, wrong side up, over the zipper and lining, aligning the top edges. Pin the layers together along the top edge.

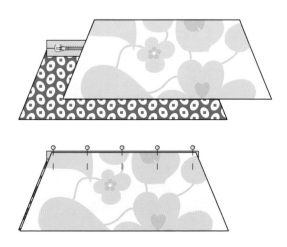

3. Using a zipper foot, sew through all the layers along the top edge of the zipper, as close to the teeth as possible, backstitching at the beginning and end. Press the outer-bag and lining pieces up and away from the zipper (gently pulling the fabric away from the zipper while using the point of your iron works well here).

4. Repeat steps 2 and 3 with the remaining outer-bag and lining pieces on the opposite side of the zipper, making sure the sides are aligned with the previous half.

5. Unzip the zipper halfway. You will be turning the bag inside out through the open zipper, so you don't want to forget this step.

6. Bring the outer-bag pieces right sides together; pin along the raw edges. Repeat with the lining rectangles. Make sure the zipper is folded evenly at both ends.

7. Sew around the perimeter of the entire piece, leaving a 3" gap along the bottom edge of the lining. Go very slowly over the zipper tape at each end,

stopping and using the hand wheel for a few stitches to make sure you don't sew over any zipper teeth. After sewing around the entire perimeter, carefully go over the zipper areas one more time for added strength. Trim around the zipper area close to the seam allowance.

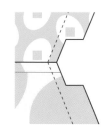

8. With wrong sides out, iron the bottom corners of the lining and outer case flat as shown. Measure 1" from each corner and draw a line perpendicular to the seam. Sew along this line on both corners of the lining and outer case. Trim ½" from the stitching line.

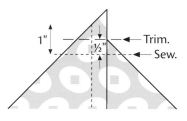

9. Turn the lining right side out through the gap, and sew the gap closed. Pull the outer case through the opening in the zipper. Push the lining into the outer case.

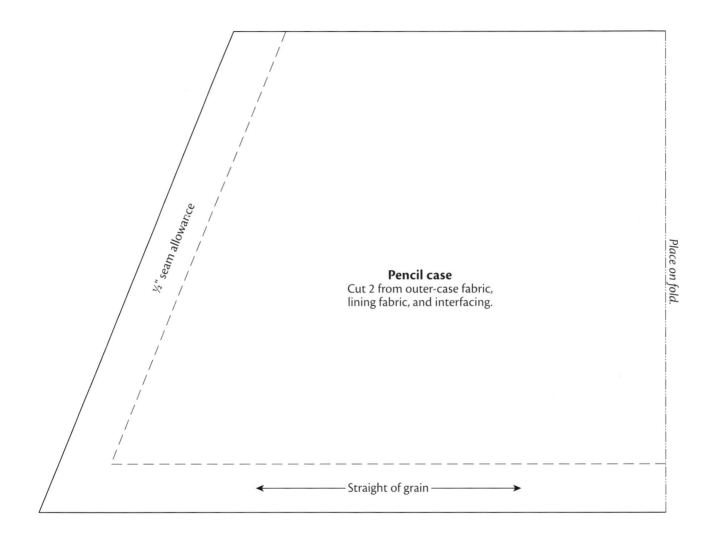

Pencil case
Cut 2 from outer-case fabric,
lining fabric, and interfacing.

½" seam allowance

Place on fold.

Straight of grain

all business laptop sleeve

Mean business without being boring. With all the gorgeous fabric available, skip the dull laptop cases and go with a hand-made, personalized sleeve as drool-worthy as the equipment inside it. For the outside of this sleeve I used Amy Butler's home-decor weight fabric, though regular cotton or cotton canvas would also work great. If you're ambitious, appliqué a design to the outer fabric before constructing the sleeve.

This sleeve is sized for a 13" Macbook (13" x 9" x 1¼"). A slightly smaller laptop will still fit, though anything more than ½" wider will be snug, and larger than 1" wider won't fit. Instructions for measuring and adjusting the pattern for a different-sized laptop are found at the end of the instructions.

This sleeve is a bit tricky because there are so many layers. Normally you don't want a lot of seam bulk, but in this case it will help protect the laptop.

MATERIALS

Yardage is based on 42" fabric. If you fussy cut, you will need more fabric.

⅝ yard of pink-and-green home-decor weight print for outer sleeve

⅝ yard of pink print for lining

1¼ yards of batting

½ yard of heavyweight interfacing, such as Pellon Decor-Bond

3" of 1½"-wide Velcro

CUTTING

Use the pattern on page 74 to make the flap template.

From the outer-sleeve print, cut:
2 rectangles, 11½" x 16½"
1 flap piece

From *each* of the lining fabric and interfacing, cut:
2 rectangles, 11" x 16"
1 flap piece

From the batting, cut:
4 rectangles, 11" x 16"
2 flap pieces

MAKING THE SLEEVE

Use ½"-wide seam allowances throughout.

1. Layer all five flap pieces as follows: interfacing; one piece of batting; the outer-fabric and lining pieces placed right sides together; and then the second piece of batting. Pin, and then sew along the short and angled sides, leaving the top straight edge open. Backstitch at the beginning and end of the seam. Trim the batting from the seam allowances. Clip the corners and turn the flap right side out. Roll the seams toward the lining (page 106) and press. Stitch ¼" from the raw edge to hold all layers together.

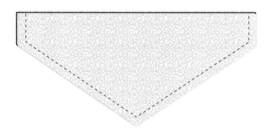

2. Place the lining rectangles right sides together and add a batting piece to the top and bottom of the stack and pin. Stitch around the two short sides and the bottom of the lining, leaving a 6" gap on one side. Trim the batting from the seam allowances. Clip the corners.

3. Layer the outer-sleeve pieces, the remaining batting pieces, and the two interfacing pieces as follows: one piece of interfacing, one piece of batting, the outer-fabric pieces (right sides together), the second piece of batting, and finally the second piece of interfacing. Stitch around the two short sides and the bottom as in step 2, except do not leave a gap. Trim the batting from the seam allowances. Clip the corners and turn the piece right side out.

4. Place the outer sleeve inside the lining piece. Place the flap between the lining and the outside bag, matching the top raw edges. Make sure the lining side of the flap is against the lining.

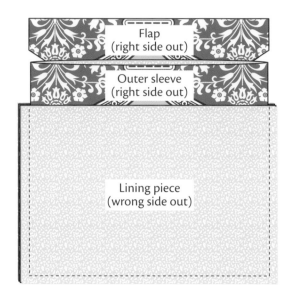

5. Stitch all the way around the top edge. Turn right side out through the gap in the lining. Sew the gap closed, roll the top seam toward the lining (page 106), and press.

6. Sew one half of the Velcro to the underside of the flap and the other half to the outside of the sleeve in the corresponding location, stitching around and through the piece as shown.

MAKING A CUSTOM SLEEVE

Laptops come in a variety of dimensions, and yours may vary in size from mine. Here's how to measure your computer so you can still create a sleeve that fits.

1. Measure the length, width, and depth of your laptop (the 13" Macbook measures 9" x 13" x 1¼").

2. Add the depth to the width (13" + 1¼" = 14¼"). From this point, when I say *width*, I mean this new number.

3. For the outer fabric, add 2¼" to the *width* of the laptop and 2½" to the *length* (this includes ½" seam allowances) (14¼ + 2¼" = 16½"; 9" + 2½ = 11½").

4. For the lining, batting and interfacing, add 1¾" to the width of the laptop and 2" to the *length* (this includes ½" seam allowances) (14¼" + 1¾" = 16"; 9" + 2" = 11")

5. For the flap, you'll need to redraw the triangle shape, but we'll keep it easy and just adjust the width. To figure out how wide the bottom of the triangle needs to be, subtract 1½" from your cut width of the outer pieces (16½" – 1½" = 15", which is the width of the 13" Macbook flap template). On a piece of template plastic or pattern paper, draw a rectangle that is this width by 7" (the height of the flap template).

    Note: For large laptops, a 7"-long flap may look too short. Feel free to extend the flap so it's longer than 7", keeping the depth measurement (2" in our example) the same. So instead of 2" of depth and 5" of "point,"

you might have 6" of point. Use scrap paper cut to different flap shapes and choose the measurement that looks the best to you.

6. Mark the center of the top edge of the rectangle. On either side, mark 2" from the bottom corners. This is the point of your triangle. Draw two lines from the 2" marks to the triangle point.

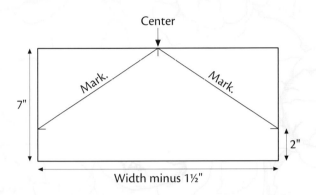

7. This template includes a ½" seam allowance, so once you cut out your new flap template, you're ready to go.

Example:

So, for a hypothetical laptop that measures 10" x 15" x 2", you would end up with:

Width = 15" + 2" = 17"

Length = 10"

Outer pieces: cut 19¼" x 12½"

Lining, batting, and interfacing: cut 18¾" x 12"

For the flap: Adjust the width to 17¾" wide at the widest point

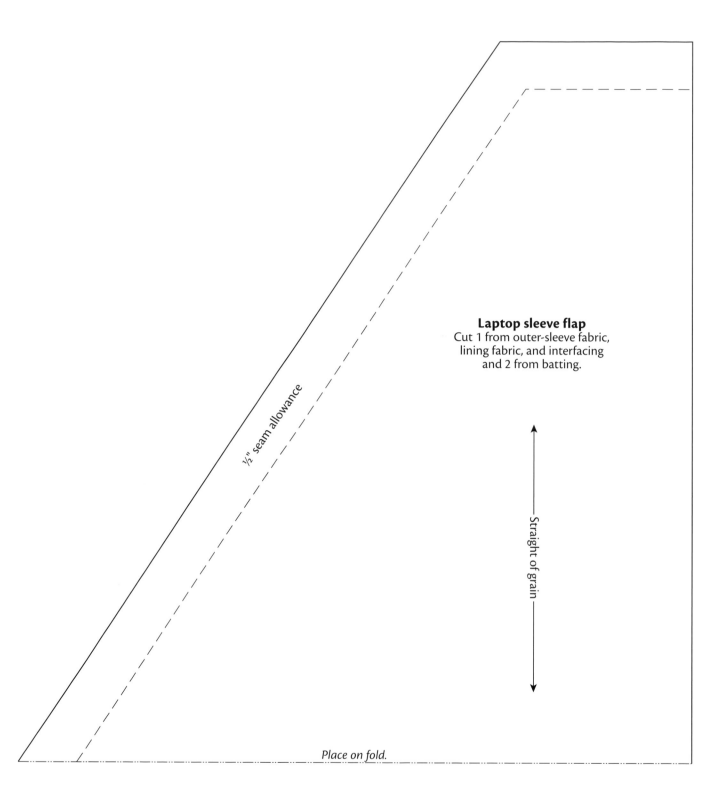

Laptop sleeve flap
Cut 1 from outer-sleeve fabric,
lining fabric, and interfacing
and 2 from batting.

½" seam allowance

Straight of grain

Place on fold.

abroad

A kitchen essential, a pot holder (along with a matching oven mitt, page 83) makes a great house-warming gift. These two projects also serve as easy introductions to basic quilting techniques. Both use a machine-stitched binding for a fast finish. A note on the machine binding instructions: I give instructions for general machine bindings (page 109), but I wrote separate instructions here because you start and end the binding differently in this particular case, to account for the loop.

Feel free to use a different block instead of the basic Four Patch. You could also appliqué a 100% wool felt or cotton motif to a single 9" square of fabric, or use the leftover strip-pieced material from the oven mitt to make a strippy pot holder. As long as you end up with two 9" x 9" squares of fabric, you can do whatever you want.

pot holder

MATERIALS

Yardage is based on 42"-wide fabric. Note that for safety, your fabric must be cotton.

⅓ yard of orange cotton print for binding

¼ yard or fat quarter of cotton fruit print for block and back

¼ yard, fat quarter, or scrap at least 4½" x 9" of cotton green print for block

¼ yard or 9" x 9" scrap of 22½"-wide insulated batting*

¼ yard or 9" x 9" scrap of 100%-cotton or wool batting*

*If you are making the pot holder and the matching oven mitt, purchase ⅞ yard of insulated batting and ⅓ yard of cotton or wool batting.

CUTTING

From the green print, cut:
2 squares, 4½" x 4½"

From the orange print, cut:
1 strip, 2" x 42"

From the fruit print, cut:
2 squares, 4½" x 4½"
1 square, 9" x 9"

From *each* of the insulated and cotton or wool battings, cut:
1 square, 9" x 9"

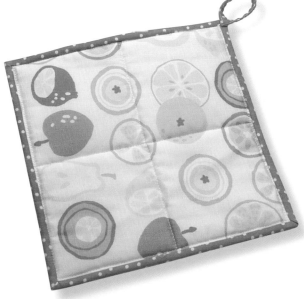

MAKING THE POT HOLDER

Use ¼"-wide seam allowances throughout.

1. With right sides together, sew each green square to a fruit square along one side. Press the seam allowance flat as sewn, and then press it to one side.

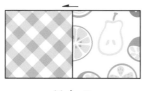

Make 2.

2. Lay out the two pairs of squares so the prints are opposite each other. Pin and sew the pairs right sides together along the long edges. Because the seam allowances were pressed in opposite directions, they should nest together and line up neatly on the right side. Press the seam allowance flat as you sew, and then press it to one side.

 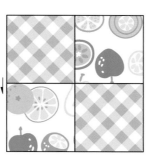

3. Create your "quilt sandwich." Place the fruit print 9" square wrong side up. Place the batting square and the insulated batting square over the fruit print square. Center the patchwork square over the batting right side up. Use either curved safety pins or large basting stitches to hold the layers together.

4. With matching thread in the top and bobbin (you might want to use two threads, one to match the top fabrics and one to match the bottom, or you could just choose a color that coordinates with both the top and bottom), quilt the layers together, using the "stitch in the ditch" method and a walking foot if you have one. Stitching in the ditch means straight stitching right along the line of the seam. Start from the edge (there should be a bit of extra batting around the edges), go slowly, and keep an eye on the needle. Stitch both seams from edge to edge.

5. Trim the excess batting and backing even with the sides of the pieced top and make sure everything is nice and square.

BINDING THE POT HOLDER

1. Press the orange 2" x 42" strip in half, wrong sides together. Starting at one corner, pin the binding around the edge of the pot holder, matching raw edges. Pin all the way around until you reach the starting corner.

2. Using a scant ¼" seam allowance, sew the binding to the pot holder, referring to the binding instructions (page 109) to miter the corners. When you reach the starting corner, overlap the binding as shown, ending your stitches at the edge of the pot holder.

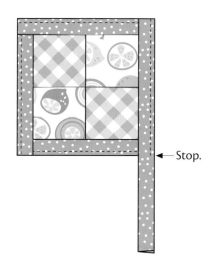

← Stop.

3. Trim the binding tail to 5". Press under ¼" to the wrong side on the binding end. Fold over the binding to the back side and secure it with pins, folding and pinning the tail to match the binding.

Press end up ¼".

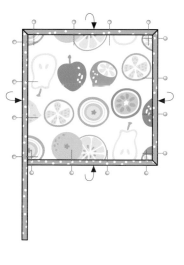

4. Sewing from the back side and starting where the binding overlaps itself, stitch right along the edge of the binding as shown, and continue sewing until you reach the end of the tail.

5. Loop the tail around so that it's perpendicular to the starting point, and tack it down by taking several stitches back and forth through all the layers.

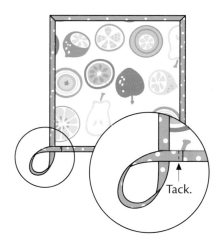

Tack.

oven mitt

If you want to make a matching strippy pot holder, purchase yardage and cut strips 30" long rather than the 14" length indicated in the cutting instructions. Use the leftover strip-pieced unit to make the pot holder (page 79).

For a really quick gift, forgo the strip piecing, cut two (mirror-image) outer mitt pieces, and skip the quilting.

MATERIALS

Yardage is based on 42"-wide fabric. Note that for safety, your fabric must be cotton.

Fat quarter or ⅓ yard of orange cotton print for pieced front, loop, and binding

Fat quarter or ⅓ yard of green plaid cotton print for pieced front

Fat quarter or ⅓ yard of fruit cotton print for back

Fat quarter or ⅓ yard of green cotton print for lining

⅞ yard of 22½"-wide insulated batting*

⅓ yard of 100%-cotton or wool batting*

*Yardages are enough to cut the batting pieces for the pot holder as well as the oven mitt.

CUTTING

Enlarge the pattern (page 85) as indicated and then make a template for cutting the mitt pieces from the enlarged pattern. Mark an "R" on the back of the template so you know which side is the reverse.

From the green plaid cotton print, cut:
1 strip, 1½" x 14"
1 strip, 2" x 14"
1 strip, 2½" x 14"
1 strip, 3" x 14"

From the orange cotton print, cut:
1 strip, 1½" x 14"
1 strip, 2" x 14"
1 strip, 2½" x 14"
1 strip, 3" x 14"
1 rectangle, 3" x 6"
1 binding strip, 2" x 12"

From the fruit cotton print, cut:
1 mitt piece, reversing the template

From the green cotton print, cut:
2 mitt pieces, reversing the template for 1 piece

From each of the insulated and cotton battings, cut:
2 mitt pieces

MAKING THE MITT

Use ¼"-wide seam allowances throughout unless otherwise indicated.

1. Lay out your strips as shown, aligning the top left corner of each strip along a straight edge (a cutting mat works great for this) so that the ends are staggered. Alternate the two fabrics in any order that looks good to you.

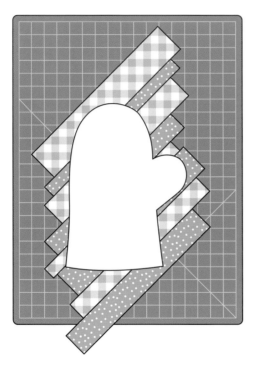

2. With right sides together, sew the strips together in the determined order to create one large piece. Press all the seam allowances toward the orange strips.

3. Using the oven mitt template, cut out one shape from the pieced fabric. If you used 30" strips so you could also make a matching pot holder, make sure you cut out the mitt shape from one corner, leaving enough room to cut a 9" x 9" square.

4. Pin or baste one piece of insulated batting and one piece of regular batting to the wrong side of the strippy mitt piece. Stitch in the ditch along all the strip seams.

5. Place the fruit print mitt piece and the strippy mitt piece right sides together, with the fruit piece on top. Mark the approximate starting and ending point of each seam of the strippy piece onto the fruit piece. Using the marks as a guide, draw the stitching lines on the front of the fruit piece, using a ruler and your marking tool of choice.

6. Pin or baste the second piece of insulated batting and regular batting to the wrong side of the fruit mitt piece. Stitch along the marked lines.

7. Prepare the loop by pressing the 3" x 6" orange piece in half lengthwise, wrong sides together. Unfold, turn the raw edges of the strip in to the center crease, refold on the center crease, and then press the strip. Topstitch a scant ⅛" along the long open edge.

8. Using a ¾" seam allowance and with right sides together, sew the lining pieces together, leaving the bottom edge open.

9. Fold the loop piece in half and pin it to the right side of the front mitt piece about 1¾" from the bottom edge, aligning the raw edges. Pin the front and back mitt pieces right sides together, sandwiching the loop between the layers.

1¾"

10. Using a ½" seam allowance and a walking foot, sew the front and back together to make the outer-mitt piece, leaving the bottom edge open. Reduce the stitch length as you stitch the tight curve between the thumb and the main mitt. Trim the insulated batting from the seam allowance.

11. Trim the excess seam allowance on the outer mitt to about ¼" and even narrower around the tight curve between the thumb and the top portion of the mitt. Turn the outer mitt right side out and roll the seams (page 106).

12. With wrong sides together, put the lining inside the outer mitt, matching the raw edges at the bottom open edge. Pin around the opening.

13. Referring to the instructions for machine binding (page 109), bind the open end of the oven mitt, lining up the binding seam with a side seam on the outer mitt.

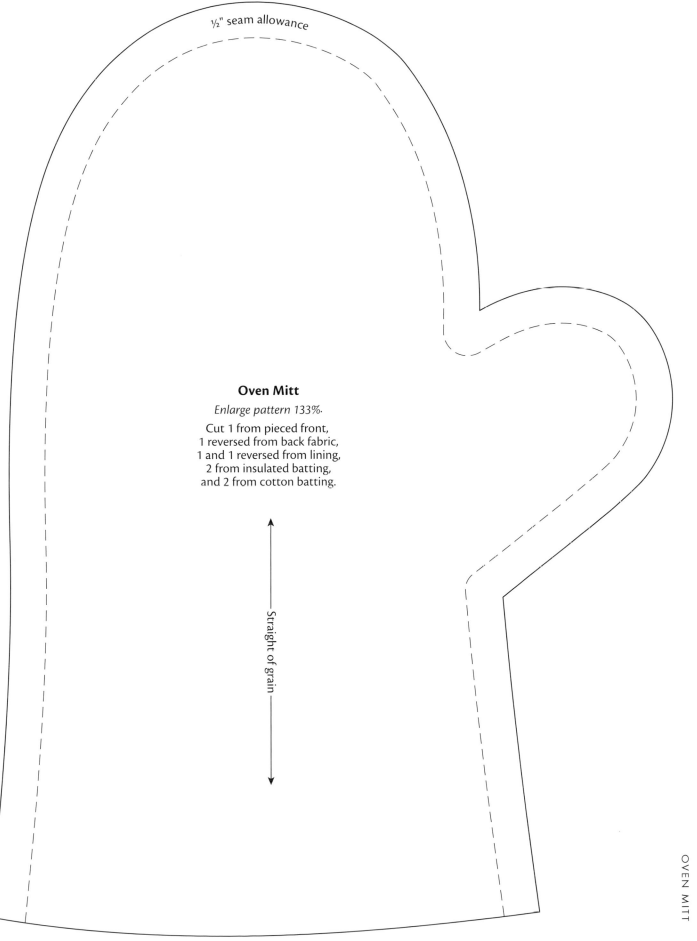

½" seam allowance

Oven Mitt

Enlarge pattern 133%.

Cut 1 from pieced front,
1 reversed from back fabric,
1 and 1 reversed from lining,
2 from insulated batting,
and 2 from cotton batting.

Straight of grain

½" seam allowance

i ❤ coffee french-press cozy

I grew up in the Seattle area, and when I was a kid I would take the bus to visit my mom downtown at work. We would get hot chocolate at the original Starbucks—this was actually a novelty before there was one on every corner. Eventually I was drinking mochas, then lattes, then drip coffee. But it wasn't until I worked at Starbucks in college that I learned what a huge difference using a French press makes in the flavor of coffee. The only problem is, even an unapologetic addict like me can't finish off a full French press before the coffee starts to get cold. With this super-easy cozy, you'll have time to gulp down that last cup while the coffee is still toasty.

MATERIALS

Fat quarter or ¼ yard of coffee-themed cotton print for outer cozy

Fat quarter or ¼ yard of brown cotton print for lining

¼ yard of insulated batting

3" piece of ¾"-wide Velcro

CUTTING

Enlarge the pattern on page 89 as indicated and then use the enlarged pattern to make a template for cutting the pieces.

From *each* of the outer fabric, lining fabric, and insulated batting, cut:

1 cozy piece

MAKING THE COZY

1. Layer the outer and lining pieces right sides together over the batting piece.

2. Using a ½"-wide seam allowance, sew around the entire piece, leaving a 3" gap along the bottom long edge. Trim the batting from the seam allowances.

3. Turn right side out, press, and stitch the gap closed.

4. Center and sew the loop side of the Velcro to the longer end of the cozy. Sew the hook side to the shorter end on the lining side in the corresponding position.

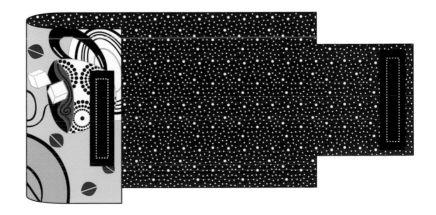

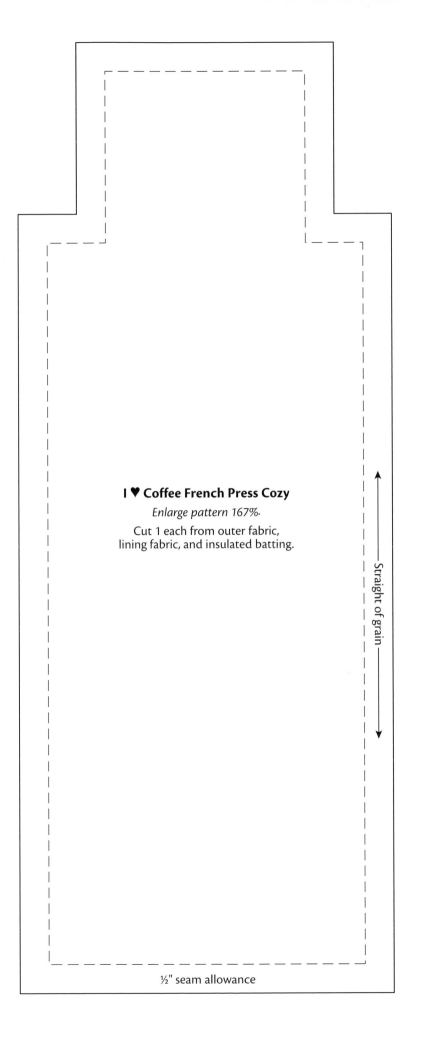

I ♥ Coffee French Press Cozy

Enlarge pattern 167%.

Cut 1 each from outer fabric,
lining fabric, and insulated batting.

Straight of grain

½" seam allowance

pocket place mats

A cute addition to the dining room table, a set of these place mats would also be really handy for a picnic. And if you've got kids around at dinnertime, the fun pocket just might make it easier to get help setting the table.

MATERIALS (FOR FOUR PLACE MATS)

Yardage is based on 42"-wide fabric.

2 yards of blue print for front, back, and pocket

½ yard of dark red print for pocket background

1 yard of low-loft batting

CUTTING

From the blue print, cut:
4 rectangles, 15" x 20"

4 rectangles, 14" x 15"

4 rectangles, 7" x 12"

From the dark red print, cut:
4 rectangles, 7" x 15"

From the batting, cut:
4 rectangles, 15" x 20"

MAKING THE PLACE MATS

Use ½"-wide seam allowances throughout.

1. Press a 7" x 12" blue piece in half, wrong sides together, to make a 7" x 6" rectangle.

2. Using matching thread, topstitch ¼" along the fold.

3. Position the pocket on a dark red rectangle, right sides facing up and bottom raw edges aligned. With right sides together, layer a blue 14" x 15" piece on top of the pocket piece, matching the short edge of the blue piece to the long edge of the pocket piece. Pin along the left edge, and then sew the seam. Press the seam allowance open.

4. Place the front unit and blue 20" x 15" piece right sides together. Place the batting piece on top.

5. Using a walking foot if you have one, sew around the entire piece, leaving a 4" gap along the bottom edge.

6. Turn right side out through the gap, roll the seams to the back (page 106), press, and stitch the gap closed.

7. Quilt ¼" around the inside perimeter of the main panel and around the inside perimeter of the pocket panel. I highly recommend using a walking foot here, but if you don't have one, use lots of curved safety pins before you begin stitching to baste the layers together to keep them from shifting. Quilt the main panel within the ¼" border, marking diagonal lines at a 45° angle and 2" apart.

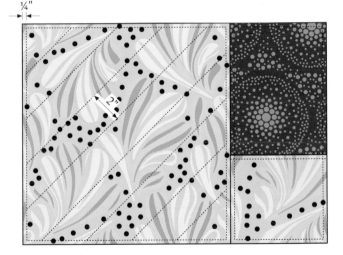

pretty crafty apron

I'm the kind of person who will pick up something in one area of my apartment, think of something else I have to find, and leave the first item wherever I go to pick up the second item (this is why I've found my car keys in my bathroom cupboard). One day, after spending half an hour searching for a roll of tape I had set down somewhere, it struck me—I seriously needed a utility apron. Whether I'm working on a painting, a sewing project, or just hanging pictures on the wall (and doing my best to misplace the hammer), I can just shove the items I'm using into the apron pockets and they're always at hand.

MATERIALS

Yardage is based on 42"-wide fabric.

⅔ yard of large-scale floral print for front and back

⅔ yard of small-scale bird print for pocket

½ yard of orange striped fabric for pocket trim and tie

CUTTING

From the large-scale floral print, cut:
2 rectangles, 12½" x 21"

From the small-scale bird print fabric, cut:
2 strips, 6½" x 21"

From the orange striped fabric, cut:
2 strips, 6" x 41"
1 strips, 2" x 21"

MAKING THE APRON

1. To make the pocket unit, using a ¼" seam allow-ance and matching the 21"-long edges, sew the orange 2" x 21" strip between the bird print 6½" x 21" strips. Press the seam allowances open.

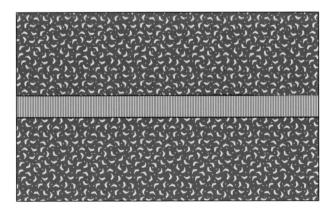

2. Press the pocket unit in half lengthwise, wrong sides together, matching the long raw edges of the brown pieces.

3. Layer the pocket unit on the right side of one of the large-scale floral rectangles, matching the bottom raw edges. Mark the pocket sections as shown,

using the marking tool of your choice. Sew on the lines through all of the layers using matching or coordinating thread.

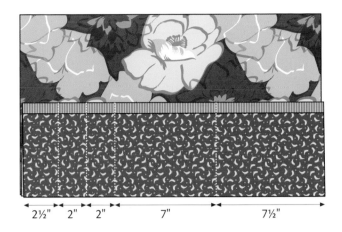

2½" ⟷ 2" ⟷ 2" ⟷ 7" ⟷ 7½"

4. Layer the remaining large-scale floral rectangle and the pocket unit right sides together, matching the raw edges. Using a ½" seam allowance, sew around the side and bottom edges, leaving the top edge open. Clip the corners, turn right side out, and press.

5. To prepare the tie, sew the two orange striped 6" x 41" strips together end to end to create an 81"-long strip. Press the strip in half lengthwise, wrong sides together. Unfold and turn the raw edges of the strip in to the center crease. On the ends of the strip, fold the corners into the center crease at a 45° angle and press. Refold the entire strip on the center crease and press the strip.

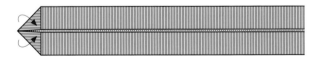

6. Fold the apron in half widthwise and finger-press the top raw edge at the center fold. Open up the tie and place it over the top edge of the apron, encasing the raw edge. Match the tie's center seam with the finger-pressed crease of the apron; pin in place. Pin the tie open edges together.

7. Using a scant ⅛" seam allowance, stitch from the open edge of the tie at one end point all the way across the apron and to the opposite end of the tie. This will close the open edges of the tie and attach it to the apron.

cotton cuff

This is an unexpected twist on the traditional leather cuff. It's super-easy, too, which means you can make one for every outfit and every mood. This is a great project for small embellishments like buttons or hot-fix crystals. When I found the blue-and-pink material for the cuff shown on page 95, I knew exactly what it needed—with glittering crystals in the eyes of the two skulls, I've unofficially nick-named it the "Goonies Never Say Die" cuff.

I usually use Velcro to fasten the cuff. Besides the ease of this method, it makes the cuff reversible. You also can use metal snaps and a snap-setting tool, but make sure to fuse or sew in an extra rectangle of heavier interfacing along with the batting to add strength where the snaps are attached.

MATERIALS

2 scraps of cotton, cotton canvas, or home-decor weight fabrics

Scrap of batting

1½" of ¾"-wide Velcro or two ½" no-sew four-part metal snaps and a snap-setting tool

Scrap of medium- to heavyweight fusible interfacing (if using snaps)

Buttons or hot-fix crystals (optional)

CUTTING

From *each* of the 2 fabrics, cut:
1 piece, 2½" x the circumference of your wrist plus 2½"

From the batting, cut:
1 piece, 2½" wide x the circumference of your wrist plus 2½"

From the interfacing (optional), cut:
2 rectangles, 1" x 2"

MAKING THE CUFF

1. If you're using snaps, fuse the interfacing rectangles to the wrong side of one of the fabric pieces, ½" from each end and centered across the width. Place the two fabric pieces right sides together and layer the batting on the bottom.

2. Using a ¼"-wide seam allowance, stitch completely around two long sides and one short side and just around the corners on the other short side. Clip the corners and turn right side out.

3. Ladder-stitch the gap closed.

4. Attach one half of the closure(s) to one end of the cuff. If you are using Velcro, position it about ¼" from the end and make sure your bottom thread matches the bottom fabric and that your top thread matches the Velcro. If you are using snaps, see "Snap Snippets" at right. Attach the other half of the closure(s) to the other end of the cuff on the opposite fabric side.

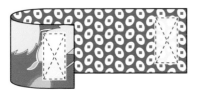

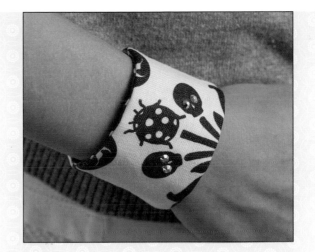

SNAP SNIPPETS

- Wrap the cuff around your wrist and mark the location of the snaps. It's helpful to have a second person mark the position of the snaps while you hold the cuff on your wrist.

- A cuff with snaps isn't reversible, so make sure you choose a "top" fabric.

VARIATION

To make a pieced version like I did with the brown-and-green cuff, simply cut irregular strips that are at least as long as the circumference of your wrist plus 2½" and piece them together using a ¼" seam allowance. Once you have a piece that is at least 3" wide, cut out your rectangle.

headband

This project is ridiculously easy. It makes a great small gift, and along the way you can whip up a variety for your own wardrobe. If you'd like a longer headband, cut three strips and piece them together to achieve the desired length. Using three pieces instead of two assures that you won't have an obvious seam in the center of the headband. Light, silky quilting cottons work very well for this project, and I used a Japanese "double gauze" for the polka-dotted headband. If you can find some, it is wonderful for a headband because it has a bit of stretch.

MATERIALS

Yardage is based on 42"-wide fabric.

¼ yard of fabric

CUTTING

From the fabric, cut:

1 strip, 4" x 42"

MAKING THE HEADBAND

1. Press the strip in half lengthwise, wrong sides together. If you establish this crease at the beginning, it makes life easier when you later turn the headband right side out.

2. Loosely fold the headband in half lengthwise, right sides together; pin along the edges, but don't press. Mark a 30°-angle line on both ends.

3. Starting at the corner of the fabric strip, sew on the marked line, pivot ¼" from the long raw edges, and then sew ¼" from the raw edges, leaving a 3" gap along the straight edge near the other end. Complete the seam, sewing on the marked line when you reach the other angled end.

4. Trim the ends ¼" from the line of stitches. Clip the points. Turn right side out through the gap, roll the seam toward the back (page 106), and press. Because the gap in this headband may encounter more tugging than other openings, I recommend you use a very small whipstitch to sew the gap closed.

Try embellishing your headband with hot-fix crystals to add a little sparkle.

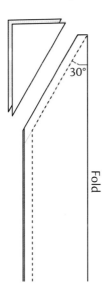

30°

Fold

knit-not scarf

I don't knit, so if I want a hand-made scarf I've got to convince one of my knitter friends to make me one. But now there's another way! With a gorgeous cotton print on one side and a soft, neck-friendly fabric on the back, this easy and sewer-friendly scarf is fast and stylish. Experiment with different kinds of fabric for the back—anything from flannel to faux fur would work great. The fringe is completely optional, of course, but I recommend adding a bit of froufrou to the ends even if you choose something besides pom-poms. For an elegant take, you could make the scarf thinner, add beaded fringe to the ends, and use velvet on the back. The scarf is also a great canvas for applique. And because it's so fast and easy to personalize, this scarf makes a great gift.

I used 54"-wide fabric for the front and back of this scarf, but if you want to use standard 42"-wide cotton, you can either make a shorter scarf or piece together two lengths of fabric.

MATERIALS

Yardage is based on 54"-wide fabric.

⅓ yard of print fabric for front

⅓ yard of coordinating fabric for back

⅝ yard of ½" pom-pom fringe (optional)

CUTTING

From the front fabric, cut:
1 strip, 9½" x 54"

From the back fabric, cut:
1 strip, 9½" x 54"

From the fringe, cut:
2 lengths, 9½"

MAKING THE SCARF

1. Pin the fringe to the right side of each end of the front strip with the pom-poms facing in.

2. With right sides together and using a ½"-wide seam allowance, sew the front and back scarf pieces together, leaving about an 8" gap along one long edge. Clip the corners, turn to the right side, and press. Sew the gap closed.

A book with such a broad range of projects is bound to draw on a variety of techniques, some you're probably familiar with and some perhaps not. For most instructions, if you're comfortable with the construction and wish to go about it a different way than I specify, please feel free. Just as I encourage personalizing projects, I also think people should use the techniques they are most comfortable with and find the most useful for them. If you're a beginner, however, I recommend following the instructions carefully to get a reliable result. I've marked each project with a skill rating from one to three flowers. You'll find that the projects in this book don't use a lot of difficult techniques, but sometimes I've rated a project higher because it has a lot of steps or is very small and not as easy to work with (such as the Portable Media Player Case on page 59, for example). Any project with a single flower rating would be a great starting point for someone new to sewing.

Below I've listed a variety of tools, techniques, and information that is important to know.

TOOLS AND SUPPLIES

Having the right tools for the job is as important for sewing as it is for painting a house or fixing a car. If you've done some sewing before, you probably have most of the tools you need already. If you're brand new to sewing, you'll want to stock up on the basics before you begin—and don't forget a container to keep it all organized. Plastic containers with lots of compartments designed for art supplies work great.

Your Machine

Most sewing machines will work just fine for these projects. You must be able to backstitch—and yes, there are some very basic machines that don't have this capability. But you'll need to backstitch, probably several times, on pretty much every project, so this feature is essential.

There are some projects where you will be sewing through many layers at a time, and the bulk beneath your presser foot will be substantial. Many machines can handle this well, but some may strain. Go slowly

through these sections, and if you still have trouble, try a stronger needle such as a jeans needle. A manual handwheel is very useful at times, like when sewing around zippers or over bulky seams.

For most projects a basic presser foot is adequate. You will find a zipper foot very useful for a few projects, and a walking foot will be helpful for any project with batting or lots of layers. A walking foot moves the top and bottom of the fabric layers at the same time, which prevents the layers from shifting and bunching as you sew. For quilted projects, like the Pocket Place Mats (page 90) or Oven Mitt (page 83), a walking foot is almost essential. If you don't have one and plan to do any sewing with batting in the future, I highly recommend the investment. You can avoid using a walking foot by using a lot of safety pins to hold your layers together (curved safety pins exactly for this purpose work the best). If you prefer, you can use long basting stitches to hold the layers together prior to quilting and remove them when you're done. Pin a lot, go slowly, and keep an eye out for fabric bunching before it becomes a problem.

Regardless of what kind of machine you have, keeping it clean and serviced will make a huge difference in its performance. If you've been sewing on batting, especially, the fibers get under the throat plate and can gum up the works.

Needle and Thread

For the sewing machine, standard Sharps will do for most projects. For any project that uses oilcloth, canvas, nylon straps, or just has a lot of layers, I recommend using a jeans needle. They are stronger and thicker to penetrate heavier fabrics. If you start to hear any needle making a "punching" sound as you sew, it's dull and needs replacing.

For hand sewing, a standard hand-sewing needle is fine. If you're having trouble getting the needle through the fabric, you may be using a needle that's too thick or has too wide of an eye. On the other hand, sometimes a needle is too delicate for the job. If you're unsure which needle will work best, you can buy a package of assorted hand-sewing needles and experiment.

I generally use high-quality cotton thread available at quilting and craft stores, like Mettler or Gütermann. For piecing projects that use several different-colored fabrics, such as the Vintage is the New Modern Patchwork Bag (page 25), use a neutral-colored thread so you don't have to change thread color often. Large spools of black, dark and light gray, dark and light cream, and white thread are always good to have on hand because they match so many fabrics. Of course, you can always use a matching-colored thread if you prefer. For topstitching and quilting, there are a variety of threads available, from basic solid cotton to metallics and color-changing variegated varieties.

Cutting Tools

Because most of my sewing skills were developed from a quilting perspective, I'm accustomed to using a rotary cutter, rotary ruler, and cutting mat. Most of the projects in the book involve rectilinear shapes, so this method works well. If you've never tried a rotary cutter, it's a great tool that can really save you time. Just make sure you keep your fingers away from the blade and use a self-healing mat under your fabric to protect your cutting surface.

Sometimes, you'll need to mark the fabric and cut out a shape using regular scissors. If you're more accustomed to cutting out pattern shapes in this way, you can cut out every pattern piece in the book with scissors. I use three types of scissors:

Those for cutting fabric, which are large and comfortable to hold. I use a pair of 8" dressmaker shears. To help keep them sharp, don't use your fabric scissors to cut anything else—and don't try to cut through a straight pin. Trust me (it was an accident...).

Those for small precision work, like cutting out appliqué designs or templates with a lot of tight curves or points. Fiskars makes the ones I use. They have very sharp 2" blades, and their oversized handles and small points give you a lot of leverage and control.

Lastly, **all-purpose, el-cheapo office scissors** that I use for everything else. Template plastic, Velcro, paper, you name it. If I'm going to abuse a pair of scissors I'd much rather do so with ones that are $5 a pack.

Besides regular scissors, you'll also want something very small and handy to snip thread, such as a pair of thread nippers—available in a variety of styles—or small embroidery scissors.

Iron

An iron is essential, and while almost any iron will do, it should have a steam feature. If not, keep a plastic spray mister handy to lightly spritz your fabric with water before you iron it. If you do have to use this method instead of steam, just be careful not to soak your fabric; you just want to get it a bit damp to get out any stubborn wrinkles, or to press open a seam.

If you're short on space, look for a mini ironing board at a bed-and-bath store, or use an insulated ironing pad. The latter is what I use, placed over an old night-stand, because there's no room in my small apartment for a standard-sized ironing board. There are also space-saving ironing boards that mount flat against the wall and are flipped down only when you need them.

Marking Tools

There seems to be as many marking tools as there are crafters. You probably have a couple that you prefer, but if you don't, see what's available at your quilting or fabric store and experiment. It often comes down to personal preference. With any marking tool, especially the "disappearing ink" variety, always test on a scrap of fabric that the mark can be removed before committing.

The marking tools I use most often are:

Clover White Heat-Soluble Marking Pen. This is a great tool for darker fabrics. Your line will take a moment to appear, but the pen creates a clean white line that disappears with heat from your iron.

Clover Blue Water-Soluble Marking Pen. This is my counterpart to the white heat-soluble pen. It draws a bright blue line that disappears with water, and it works great for lighter fabric.

Chalk pencils. There are a huge variety of chalk pencils and other chalk marking tools available. If you choose chalk, experiment to find your favorite and make sure it brushes off easily.

Transfer paper. My favorite transfer paper is Saral. It comes in several colors and is available at fabric and art stores. Saral is wax free, which means it will erase, brush off, and wash out. If you plan to mark pattern lines where they could later show, test the marks first just in case.

You can also use the traditional dressmaker's carbon paper available at fabric stores. These lines aren't removable, however, so you should only mark on the wrong side of the fabric where any marks won't show.

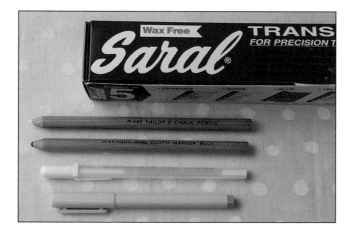

Interfacing

Interfacing is used in many of the projects in this book. Sometimes it's used to give something structure, other times it just adds a layer of protection to extend the life of your project. I usually use fusible interfacing, though sew-in interfacing works just as well.

When it comes to interfacing, my general policy is that there's "heavyweight interfacing" and everything else. What I mean by that is that if a project asks for heavyweight interfacing, it's important to use that to give the project enough structure. If the instructions ask for lightweight or mediumweight interfacing, however, there's a little more leeway and you can choose based on preference. Decor-Bond by Pellon is my go-to heavyweight interfacing. Otherwise, there is a variety of fusible interfacings available, from sheer to sturdy. I choose a middle-of-the-road interfacing for almost everything. Sometimes, though, I don't want a project to have any stiffness but want to include interfacing—a bag, for example, that will have car keys rattling around in it, and I want the interfacing to prevent the keys from eventually punching through the fabric. In these cases I'll use a lightweight interfacing.

Whichever interfacing you choose, make sure to follow the manufacturer's instructions, and for fusible interfacing, always use a Teflon pressing cloth or a piece of parchment paper to protect the surface of your iron and your fabric.

Batting

Like interfacing, batting comes in a variety of weights. You can purchase it off a large roll or in a package. The packaged batting is generally used in quilting so it comes in a variety of standard bed-quilt sizes. Aside from the dimensions, however, it's the same as batting on a roll.

I generally choose lightweight batting for the projects in this book. Most of the time I'm just looking to add a bit of body to the project, but I'm not making a fabric marshmallow. Some projects, like the All Business Laptop Sleeve (page 71), will benefit from a slightly thicker batting, while the Pocket Place Mats (page 90) would look silly with a thick, puffy batting. There are hardly ever "make-or-break" situations where your choice of batting can tank a project, however, so it's not something to stress about.

Batting comes in cotton, polyester, wool, silk, and blends. I usually choose cotton, but frankly whatever I've got laying around my apartment—as long as it's an appropriate thickness—is what I use. For quilts you have to think about warmth, weight, and even flammability (for kids' quilts) but for accessories it's generally just a matter of preference. However, if you're making something that will be around high heat, like a pot holder, you should use 100% cotton or wool.

Some projects call for insulated batting, which looks like aluminum foil sandwiched between two layers of batting. Insulated batting is great for kitchen accessories. For items that need to offer heat protection, there's no substitute.

Pins and Rulers

Pins are another tool where it's useful to have a variety on hand. Long, stiff straight pins are great for all-purpose fabric, and especially for heavier oilcloth or when you have several layers of fabric. Smaller, thinner pins are good for areas where you don't have much room to pin or for delicate fabrics you don't want to punch huge holes in, and they tend to be sharper than the big fat pins. Lastly, I keep a tin of curved safety pins around for pinning the layers of fabric and batting together when I'm preparing to quilt. These are available at quilting and fabric stores and are very useful.

Rulers and other measuring tools are, of course, absolutely necessary. Besides the ubiquitous measuring tape, I keep a variety of clear plastic rulers around in different shapes and sizes. If you decide to use a rotary-cutting tool, you'll need at least a couple of these plastic rulers—generally used for quilting—to cut against. Even if you are marking patterns and cutting with scissors, these rulers make great straight edges. The other indispensable ruler I use is a sewing and knitting gauge. It's a 6"-long, slim metal ruler with a slide marker on it. It's perfect for taking small, quick measurements as you work.

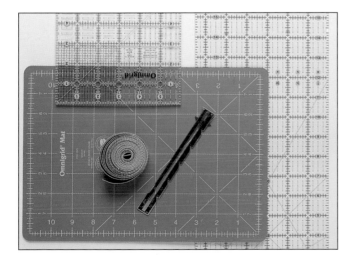

CREATING TEMPLATES

There are several projects where you will need to create templates from patterns. There are a couple of ways you can go about doing this.

Photocopy the pattern given with the project. Some of the patterns will need to be enlarged anyway and it's easiest to do this on a photocopier. Once you've made the copy, cut it out and you've got your template. Lay the template on the wrong side of the fabric and trace carefully around the edge with your chosen marking tool. If you want, you can pin the uncut template to the fabric and then cut around it, but I've never had good luck with this method; the copier paper is too stiff and I find it hard to get a precise result.

Another option, one that works very well for projects you are likely to make again (and who could resist making a French-press cozy for every coffee snob they know?) is to use template plastic. Available in sheets from quilting, fabric, and craft stores, you can trace the pattern directly onto the translucent plastic, cut it out, and have a template that can be reused endlessly and is stiff enough to easily trace around. If you decide to use template plastic, and I recommend giving it a shot, try to find the large sheets, which are commonly found at quilting stores. Craft stores sell the same stuff, but sometimes it's only available in 8½" x 11" sheets, and at several times the cost of the larger sheets. Template plastic works great for appliqué designs, because you can collect the templates as you make them and have an ever-growing stash of ready-made designs that you can use over and over again.

STITCH GLOSSARY

Throughout the projects, I'll instruct you to perform certain sewing tasks, such as sewing a gap closed or topstitching. I've given some of my favorite stitches for specific tasks in this section, but they aren't the only ones you can use. If you feel more comfortable with another stitch that suits the job, by all means use it.

Closing the Gap

Many of these projects, and most sewing projects in general, involve sewing pieces wrong sides together and then turning the finished piece to the right side. This often leaves you with a gap that you left just for turning, and the final step is to sew that gap closed. You have a few options.

By far the fastest and easiest is to machine stitch the opening closed. This method shows the stitching more than others, but for certain projects where speed and ease are more important than a more invisible stitch, you can't beat it. I recommend it when the seam is hidden, as with the lining of a bag. Remember to backstitch at the beginning and end of the seam.

Even though machine stitching is usually quicker, I generally sew all my gaps closed by hand. The two stitches shown here are my favorites. My general policy is if the gap is on the inside where it won't be seen, like on a lined bag, I whipstitch, and if it's on the outside, I ladder stitch. I'll tell you a secret, though. If you are skilled at tiny stitches and use thread that matches the fabric, no one will notice a whipstitched seam unless they're using a magnifying glass. (And who needs such picky folks, anyhow?)

Whipstich. This stitch is a favorite hand stitch of mine because it's fast, and there's something satisfying about making these tiny, regular stitches. It does show, unlike the ladder stitch, but if you use a matching thread and make very little stitches it will really fade into the project. Similar to machine stitching, however, it can make the seam "stand up" a bit, depending on the size of your stitches.

1. I always start a whipstitch by burying the knot under the machine-stitched portion of the seam, just before the area you need to whipstitch.

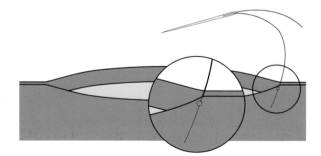

2. Make a small, diagonal stitch across the seam, insert the needle into the back, and bring it up through the front at the same point. Repeat this motion by making another diagonal stitch over to the back and gently pulling on the thread as you make each stitch to close the gap. Imagine making a "Z" shape over the seam.

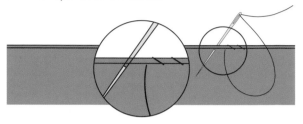

3. To finish, make several tiny stitches on top of each other and snip the thread. The smaller and shallower your stitches, the less obvious this seam will be.

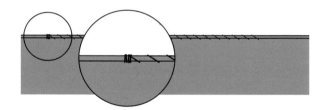

Ladder stitch. This stitch makes a great hidden seam, so it's perfect for a seam that will be visible or any outside seam that you can't sew from the inside. I use it on the ends of straps that I have to turn right side out, like the shoulder strap of the Bird-Watcher Messenger Bag (page 41) where the opening is flat and visible. The ladder stitch creates a nice flat seam and is great for seams where flatness is necessary. It's important to make small ladder stitches, because your seam may start to curve between stitches if they're too long. The ladder stitch is similar to a slip stitch, so if you're more comfortable with that, they're interchangeable for the purpose of these projects.

1. To start a ladder stitch, anchor your knot on the underside of the seam allowance on one half of the fabrics to be joined and bring the needle out through the folded edge. Insert the needle through the fold on the opposite edge and bring it out through the fold about ¼" away.

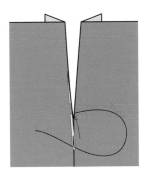

2. Insert the needle into the opposite fold directly across from where the thread emerged and take a stitch into this fold. Continue in this manner, stitching back and forth across the folds for the length of the opening and gently pulling on the thread as you make each stitch to close the gap. You should begin to see a "ladder" of stitches forming.

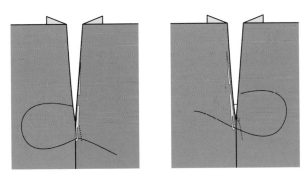

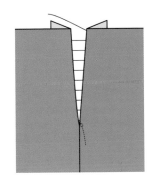

3. Anchor your thread at the end by taking several small stitches on top of each other and then snip the excess thread.

Hemming

Knowing how to make an invisible hem stitch can come in handy for many projects. I use the **blind hem stitch** to hand stitch bindings to a quilt (or a bag, pot holder, etc.)

1. Anchor your thread under the fold of your binding to hide the knot, and then bring the needle up through the front of the binding very near the edge of the fold.

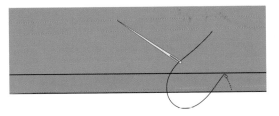

2. Insert the needle into the project backing just above where it came out at the binding. Go one stitch length and come out through the binding near the fold again. Make sure you don't make the stitch through all the layers—just catch the backing fabric.

3. Continue to repeat step 2 to make additional stitches, being careful to just catch a few threads from the binding each time (this is what makes it an invisible stitch).

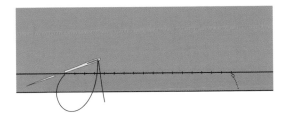

4. When you reach the end, make several small stitches through the backing fabric and the binding to anchor the thread. Bury the thread under the binding by inserting the needle under the binding and coming out somewhere in the middle of the binding; snip the thread.

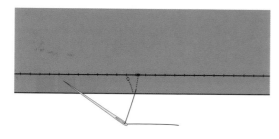

Topstitching

Topstitching means making a line of stitching "on top" of the fabric that doesn't create a seam and that shows on the finished project. Topstitching is pretty self-explanatory, but here are a few tips:

• Use a straight stitch set at a standard short to medium length.

• You can use any thread, but there are threads labeled "topstitch" that are thicker and sometimes have a bit of sheen. You're more than welcome to use thread meant specifically for topstitching, but all-purpose thread will do.

• Topstitching can be almost invisible or very visible and decorative. Sometimes you want it to disappear, and sometimes you want it to pop out. In cases where you want to really show it off, I'd recommend trying a dedicated topstitching thread.

• When topstitching around the edge of a project or along a pocket fold, sewing ⅛" away from the edge is usually just right. Oftentimes I will call for a scant ⅛", which basically means to topstitch very close to the edge. Just how close is often an aesthetic choice, so if you prefer a slightly larger space between the edge and the stitching, do so. Occasionally, however, as in the Plein Air Sketchbook Cover (page 61), a correct fit depends on a narrow topstitching margin.

• For topstitching that is right along the edge of something, I usually use one of the inner indentations on my presser foot as a guide. It works not only as a visual guide, but often helps keep the fabric "in

line" as well—very helpful when your eyes are crossing while trying to sew a straight line along the edge of a 40" strap!

ROLL YOUR WHAT NOW?

I instruct you to "roll your seams" many times throughout this book. I asked a friend who sews if she knew what that meant, and while she could guess what I was talking about she'd never heard the phrase before. So in case it's gibberish to anyone else, here's what it means.

Let's say you're attaching the lining of a bag to the outer bag; then you turn it inside out, and the seam is kind of curled up on itself, or puffy, or needs cleaning up—however you want to describe it, it doesn't look *finished*. This is when you need to literally roll the seam on a flat surface, say on an ironing board, cutting mat, or even your pant leg (jeans work great), so that the top fabric rolls slightly to the inside of the project. The more the fabric can stick to the surface, the better—if it's sliding around under your hands nothing will happen. You're trying to get the bottom fabric to "grab" the flat surface as your fingers roll the top fabric forward. It will make sense when you try it, trust me. I get a little obsessed about rolling the seams on just about anything, but it makes for a wonderful clean, finished edge.

EMBELLISHMENTS

By their nature, embellishments are almost never required, and in fact there are so many gorgeous fabrics in the world that often the fabric itself is all you need. But embellishments can add an unexpected level of detail, or take something from casual to fancy, or just personalize an accessory into something that only you could have made.

There are countless techniques for embellishment, and going through any in great detail is beyond the scope of this book, but there are a few that I use occasionally when I want something a little different.

Machine Appliqué

Appliqué opens up a lot of opportunity for design. You can create almost any shape you like using appliqué. This is what makes it so appealing and versatile. Hand appliqué is very beautiful, but there's beauty in machine appliqué as well—that of efficiency. It's faster, easier, and while the stitching generally shows more than with hand appliqué, done neatly it looks equally nice—just different. Another advantage that can't be ignored is instant gratification—you can turn a design idea into a finished appliqué in a few minutes.

There are several ways to machine appliqué, but I'll explain my preferred method of raw-edged appliqué using fusible web. This method allows for complicated designs that are easy to cut out, and the fusible web adds a bit of structure to the fabric to be appliquéd, which makes it easier to stitch. Vary the weight of the fusible web depending on the project. You may want a softer finished appliqué and would choose a light-weight fusible. Also, as with the Victorian Cameo Bag (page 21) consider that you may have several layers of fusible on top of one another.

1. To create an appliqué, first draw your design onto the paper side of a piece of fusible web, such as Wonder Under. The finished appliqué will face the opposite direction of the pattern, so if your design is directional, trace the mirror image onto the fusible. (The pattern for the horse head appliqué on the Victorian Cameo Bag on page 21 has already been reversed for the fusible-web method.) Cut roughly around your design.

2. Follow the manufacturer's instructions to fuse the rough-cut shape to the wrong side of the appliqué fabric. Use a piece of parchment paper or a Teflon pressing sheet between the ironing board and the fabric as well as the iron and the fabric to protect both your iron and your ironing board.

3. Let the fabric cool and then cut out the shape along the marked line. Once it is cut out, peel off the paper backing. Be sure the fabric is completely cooled off before trying to peel off the backing, otherwise the paper tends to stick and pull away bits of adhesive.

4. Position the design on your background fabric and fuse it in place.

5. At this point you can choose which machine stitch to use around the edge of your design. Common choices are a zigzag stitch, blanket stitch, or satin stitch. It depends on your preference and what you think will best suit the design. I usually choose a blanket stitch. For any design and any stitch, experiment on a scrap of fabric first to adjust the length and width of the stitch to best suit the design. A smaller design, or one with tight turns or sharp corners, will look best with a narrow width and short stitch length.

6. Once you've chosen and adjusted your stitch, sew around the edge of the design. Choose a straight area to begin and backstitch at the beginning and end. Put the needle in the down position and pivot the fabric to get around tricky corners; go slowly until you get the hang of it.

Other Embellishments

There are many other ways to spice up a project. Remember the BeDazzler rhinestone setter from the 1970s and '80s? Well, there's a new tool called a hot-fix applicator wand or "glitzer" that might make you remember those old infomercials—I sure did—but this is actually a tool you'd want to use. You use the small tool to heat the glue on the back of tiny crystals and affix them to fabric, either scattering them randomly or creating a pattern. The crystals come in a variety of colors, and their small size means the result is subtle—as long as you don't go overboard. The effect works best when you add just a bit of sparkle, not serious bling. There are several different versions of the wand available, and you can probably find one at your local craft store. If not, do an online search for "hot-fix applicator wand" and you'll have many options at your fingertips.

Like *glitz*, the word *fringe* makes me a bit anxious. But trust me when I say that anytime I recommend fringe, I am *not* talking about tacky leather jackets or those horrible handbags with fringe as long as the bag itself. There is a wide variety of fringe out there comprised of anything from graceful beads to strings of little tiny pom-poms.

Speaking of beads, if you have a bead stash you can sew them to a project, use them to make a little handmade fringe, or make a unique zipper pull.

In a similar vein, buttons in any shape, color, and size can be added to any project. I'm a big fan of using buttons to cover up the stitching from applying Velcro. This also gives the impression of a button closure without all the work of making a buttonhole. You can see this embellishment on one Cotton Cuff (page 95). Speaking as someone who has way more crafting supplies than I have room for, I hesitate to encourage more hoarding, but I recently discovered the joy of a button stash and highly recommend the practice. Antique buttons are easily available at flea markets and craft shows, though I'm always picking up new buttons at fabric and craft stores as well.

MACHINE QUILTING

Machine quilting at its most basic is the process of sewing through layers of fabric and batting to hold those layers together. Generally speaking, there's a layer of batting sandwiched between two layers of fabric. Quilting by hand or machine has been done for hundreds of years to hold layers of cloth together, but folks learned early on it could be decorative as well.

Machine quilting can be as simple as straight lines, as seen in the projects in this book, or as complex as floral patterns, swooping feathers, leaves, or even pictorial designs. I only cover straight-line quilting here; free-motion quilting is great fun, but the technique has filled entire books. I highly recommend grabbing one and experimenting. Just make sure you experiment on scraps first!

 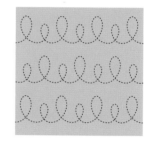

Straight-line quilting   Free-motion quilting

Machine quilting and free-motion quilting offer different opportunities for design.

Straight-line machine quilting is really easy. Using a walking foot makes it as simple as a straight seam, though for these smaller projects you can probably get away without a walking foot if you want (but it's an important investment if you plan on doing much quilting). If you don't use a walking foot, you'll need to use a lot of pins or basting stitches and be very careful that the fabric layers aren't bunching and sliding around as you sew.

1. Use the marking tool of your choice to mark the quilting lines on the top or outer fabric.

2. Lay the top and bottom fabric layers wrong sides together with the batting in between. Use curved safety pins or long stitches to temporarily baste the layers together.

3. Pick a thread that looks nice against your top fabric (whether it stands out against the fabric or blends in is up to you) and set your machine for a medium-length straight stitch. Stitch on the marked lines. At the beginning and end of a line of stitching, you can either backstitch, or make about ½" of very short stitches, which is a bit more hidden and is a more common quilting method.

BINDING

Binding is necessary to enclose the raw edges of a quilted project. These instructions encompass how to make mitered corners on square projects, like the Pot Holder (page 79). For projects like the Oven Mitt (page 83) where you will only cover one continuous edge, skip step 3. Cut binding strips 2" wide across the width of the fabric, and use a walking foot or pin liberally.

1. Press your binding strip in half lengthwise, wrong sides together.

2. Lay the binding flat on the front of the project with the raw edges aligned; pin in place along one edge. For projects like the Oven Mitt (page 83) where the binding seam should align with the mitt seam, place the end of the binding so it extends ½" beyond the seam. Begin sewing several inches from the end of the binding using a ¼" seam allowance. For square projects, stop stitching ¼" from the first corner and backstitch; for other projects, stop stitching several inches from the beginning tail and proceed to step 4.

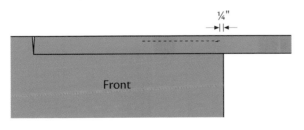

3. Fold the end of the binding up at a 90° angle to make a 45°-angle fold. Then fold the binding straight down, aligning the raw edges with the raw edges of the next side to be sewn. Start stitching at the fold, backstitch, and continue sewing the binding to that side. Stop sewing ¼" from the corner and repeat the folding technique. Continue around the remaining sides of the project.

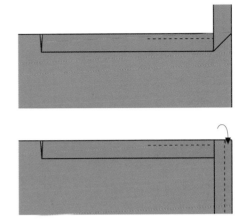

4. Once you've sewn almost all the way around, stop a few inches before your starting point. Lay your two binding tails flat against the quilt edge and overlap them ½"; trim off the excess.

5. Open up the binding and place the tails right sides together. Join them with a ¼" seam. Press the seam allowance open.

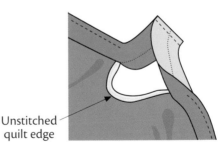

Unstitched quilt edge

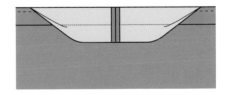

6. Refold the binding in half and finish stitching the binding to the project using a ¼" seam allowance.

7. Fold the binding over to the back of the project, just covering the first line of stitching. Use metal hair clips or pins to secure it in place.

8. When you reach a corner, fold over the first side completely, and then fold over the second side. This will miter the corner.

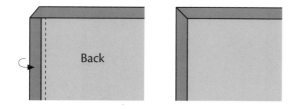

9. Use a blind hem stitch (page 105) to secure the binding to the quilt back, or refer to "Machine-Stitched Binding" at right to stitch it in place by machine.

MACHINE-STITCHED BINDING

Machine-stitched bindings aren't as invisible as hand-stitched binding, but they are definitely quick and easy. I prefer to use a machine-stitched binding for fast little projects, like the Pot Holder and Oven Mitt. If it's a gift, however, and assuming I have time (me, procrastinate?), I'll always use a hand-stitched binding.

Attach the binding to the project as described in steps 1–8 beginning on page 109, using straight pins to secure the binding after you have folded it to the back of the project. Pick a top and bottom thread that match, respectively, the back and front of your quilt. Using two threads is optional, of course, but both will show to some degree. Sewing from the back of the quilt where the binding's folded edge is held down with pins, topstitch right along the folded edge, backstitching at the beginning and end. When you reach a corner, insert the needle into the mitered fold, pivot, and continue stitching.

PROJECT CARE AND CLEANING

Before you start to work on a project in this book, you'll want to consider how to take care of it when it's finished. You certainly don't want to spend time, money, and effort on a handmade item just to let it sit unused because of a little dirt.

To prewash your fabric or not is a never-ending debate in the quilting community. Garment sewers might consider the answer obvious, because unless you're working with especially delicate fibers you're going to wash the piece of clothing once it's made, no question, so prewashing is necessary. But what if you don't see yourself washing a project, or are unsure?

My basic rule of thumb for any handmade item is that if you know you'll be tossing the finished project into the wash at some point, prewash the fabric. If you know the most you'll ever do is gently sponge off a smudge or two, prewashing isn't necessary. If you're unsure, go ahead and prewash. I like the crisp feel of new, unwashed cotton, so unless I know I'll be washing the finished project, I skip prewashing.

Some examples of projects I recommend prewashing the fabrics for are the Pocket Place Mats (page 90), Pot Holder and Oven Mitt (pages 79 and 83), and the I ❤ Coffee French-Press Cozy (page 87). Examples of project I wouldn't worry about prewashing the fabrics for are the Flea Market Purse (page 27), Evening Essentials Wristlet (page 51), and Portable Media Player Case (page 59).

If you do prewash and would like to add back some of that stiffness (which will prevent the fabric from stretching as much when you sew), try using spray starch or spray sizing, available at fabric and craft stores. For projects that you can't just throw in the wash, like those with store-bought handles or interfacing (anything but sheer tends to pucker if you wash it), you have a couple of options. One is to simply wipe the project clean with a damp sponge or hand wash it in cold water and let it air dry. Keep in mind that anything you wash might have to be ironed afterward.

The other option is to prevent the dirt in the first place by using Scotchgard or a similar product. I've stayed away from Scotchgard in the past because it always seemed like a pretty nasty chemical spray, but it's been reformulated to be less harmful to people and the environment, and frankly there just aren't other options that work nearly as well. So if you do want to protect a project by using a spray like Scotchgard, just make sure to apply it outside or in a well-ventilated area.

about the author

Cassie Barden has been involved in making art her whole life, from cartooning, filmmaking, and painting to making odd stuffed animals and creating costumes for Burning Man and Halloween. An interest in both sewing and fashion inspired her to start creating her own one-of-a-kind bags and accessories that appeal to both her utilitarian and style-conscious natures. She lives and works in a charming and rickety studio apartment in Capitol Hill, an eclectic, vibrant neighborhood of Seattle with its own unique fashion sense. When she's not sewing, Cassie enjoys two Seattle institutions: live music and drinking coffee. A graphic designer for Martingale & Company, she is inspired by contemporary art and design, anything retro or old-fashioned, and Seattle's urban culture.

Visit her website at www.thenewhandmade.com.